THE
GLASGOW
GRAVEYARD
GUIDE

JIMMY BLACK

SAINT ANDREW PRESS
1992

First published in 1992 by
SAINT ANDREW PRESS
121 George Street, Edinburgh EH2 4YN

Copyright © 1992 Jimmy Black

ISBN 0 7152 0670 2

British Library in Cataloguing Publication Data
Black, Jimmy
Glasgow Graveyard Guide
I. Title
929.50941443

ISBN 07152-0670-2

Design concept and **maps** by Mark Blackadder.
Cover photographs by Paul Turner.
Etchings from Peter Mackenzie's *Curious and
Remarkable Glasgow Characters,* Glasgow, 1891;
Samuel G Green's *Scottish Pictures,* London 1891;
Cassell's *Old and New Edinburgh,* James Grant,
1887; Hutton's *Literary Landmarks of Edinburgh,*
London 1891.

Printed and **bound** by
Athenaeum Press Ltd, Newcastle upon Tyne.

CONTENTS

The Author wishes to acknowledge, with grateful thanks, those people who provided him with, as they say in Glasgow, 'great dods o help', in the preparation of this book:

BILL BRODIE, Glasgow Cathedral guide; MARY CALDWELL, who walks her dog in the Southern Necropolis; PADDY DALY, Catholic Press Office; ANNE DOCHERTY, Scottish Film Archive; CALLUM ENGLISH, eagle-eyed searcher; GORDON ENGLISH, hawk-eyed searcher; ANNE ESCOTT and the STAFF, Glasgow Room, Mitchell Library; MARGARET FERGUSON, Glasgow historian; CHARLOTTE HUTT, Southern Necropolis Historical Survey; SYLVIA JAMIESON, Strathclyde Theatre Group; ALEX LINTON of Cathcart Cemetery; CATHY McFARLANE of Glasgow District Council, Cemeteries Department; JOHN NEIL, Secretary, Glasgow Battalion, Boys' Brigade; SANDRA PINKERTON, Springboig Library; IRENE PYLE, People's Palace Museum; ELIZABETH REOCH, Eastwood District Council; DUNCAN SHIELDS, Cathcart; ANDY STUART, Springburn Museum; DAVIE THOMSON, St Peter's Cemetery; THOMAS WAUGH, Shettleston historian.

ACCESS TO GRAVEYARDS

GLASGOW CATHEDRAL (1123)	Cathedral Square
Old Churchyard	Cathedral Square
New Churchyard (1801)	Cathedral Square
NECROPOLIS (1832)	Cathedral Square
ST DAVID'S (RAMSHORN)	Ingram Street
Old Burying Ground (1720)	Ingram Street
New Burying Ground (1780)	Ingram Street
Crypt (1825)	Ingram Street
SIGHTHILL (1840)	Springburn Road
SOUTHERN NECROPOLIS (1840)	Caledonian Road
CALTON (1786)	Abercromby Street
JOCELYN SQUARE	Saltmarket
GORBALS (1715)	Old Rutherglen Rd
WESTERN NECROPOLIS (1882)	Tresta Road
ST PETER'S (DALBETH) (1851)	London Road
CATHCART (1876)	Brenfield Road
ST KENTIGERN'S (1882)	Balmore Road

Most of the city's graveyards are administered by Glasgow District Council Parks and Recreation (Cemeteries and Crematoria). However, Glasgow Cathedral burying grounds are administered by the Cathedral; the Ramshorn Crypt is part of the church owned by the University of Strathclyde; St Peter's (Dalbeth) is administered by the Archdiocese of Glasgow; and Cathcart Cemetery is run by Eastwood District Council.

INTRODUCTION

Death has always been as fatal in Glasgow as it is anywhere else. However, sober students of 'Glasgowness' seem to agree that there is a distinctive 'Glasgow' attitude towards the phenomenon of death. They will tell you that something of the quality of this attitude may be discerned in the old Glasgow story of two housewives meeting in Argyle Street. Their conversation went thus:

Jenny: 'Haw, Hilda! Hello! Hivny seen ye since tauties were fourpence a stane. How's yer man, Erchie?'

Hilda: 'Aw, Jenny, it's you ... Erchie? Died three months ago .... '

Jenny: 'Awa tae Hell! .... '

It has to be explained to those unfamiliar with the Glasgow idiom that Jenny's exclamation of anguish is not a comment on the ultimate destination of Erchie's soul!

The visitor taking the journey through the graveyards of Glasgow will surely become aware of a special Glasgow con-dition—apart, that is, from the common condition of deadness. It is experienced when he or she imbibes that odd mixture in the atmosphere—elements of the sad, the arrogant, the courageous, the right-eous, the dreadful and hilarious, blended in unique proportions, and to be quaffed and enjoyed when taken with the stories of some of the occupants of those quiet places.

The journey is a heady experience wending past the resting places of St Mungo's bones ... Maister Peter Lowe, surgeon extraordinaire ... John Henry Alexander, actor-manager credited with inventing the Great Gun Trick in which the trickster catches a bullet in his mouth ... past the grave of Pierre Emile L'Angelier, allegedly poisoned by Madeleine Smith ... and past the grave of Benny Lynch, World Flyweight Boxing Champion.

I do hope that my choice of graveyards catches the fancy and stirs the imagination of those who follow the trail. Remember, though, Glasgow graveyards are no safer than those of any other city. Never walk alone!

Jimmy Black 1992

GLASGOW CATHEDRAL

Long, long before the Necropolis was opened to become Glasgow's answer to the Pere Lachaise in Paris, upper-crust Glaswegians preferred to be interred in the precincts of the Cathedral (1123). A chosen few even attained the distinction of being buried *inside* the Cathedral. And, in there, they became part of an exclusive gathering hosted by the patron saint of the city himself—St Kentigern, more fondly known as Mungo. This tour therefore starts with the top men.

Down in the crypt, the tomb of {1} **ST MUNGO** takes centre stage. The shrine, under a heavy four-pillared canopy, has a rich carpet spread over it, the gift of a Dr Hepburn, costing some £25,000. It had previously been stretched under the coronation thrones of Edward VII and George V in Westminster Abbey. An overhead light casts a strange eeriness over the scene.

Mungo, the illegitimate son of the King of Lothian's daughter, left Culross where he had been reared by the monks of St Serf, and lived for a while with the venerable Fergus in Carnoch, Stirlingshire.

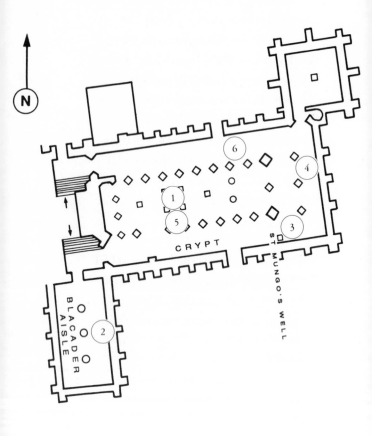

N

BLACADER AISLE

CRYPT

ST MUNGO'S WELL

1

2

3

4

5

6

GLASGOW CATHEDRAL

Abbot Fergus, on his death bed, said something like this to Mungo: 'When I die, place my body on a cart. Hitch two bullocks to the cart and let them wander westwards ... Wherever they stop, make that my burying place .... '

Those two bullocks certainly made a fair old journey of it: they did not stop until they reached the green slopes of the Molendinar Glen, probably to slake their thirst in the burn. Wasn't it convenient too that, after a non-stop journey of some forty-odd miles, those animals should halt just below the hill where St Ninian had created a cemetery almost two hundred years earlier?

Mungo buried his old abbot up on the hill and legend tells that his bones are somewhere near the Blacader Aisle on the south side of the crypt.

Being in such venerable company would surely have pleased {2} **KIRKMAN FINLAY**, who is there in that very Aisle. A brass tablet on the wall tells just a little of this remarkable man: 'In memory of Kirkman Finlay, Esqu. of Castle Toward who died on the 14th March, 1842, in the 70th year of his age and is buried in this Aisle. He represented the Glasgow District of Boroughs in the parliament which was elected in 1812 and he was chosen Lord Provost of Glasgow the same year.'

But there was a lot more to Kirkman. He was Britain's top entrepreneurial cotton merchant in the early years of the nineteenth century and sent the first trading ship to India. Indeed, he broke the monopoly at that time of the East India Company.

Kirkman stood again for parliament in the May 1831 election. His opponent was Joe Dixon of the famous iron-smelting company on Glasgow's Southside—known locally as Dixon's Blazes.

Electoral reform was in the air, but Kirkman was no reformer! Moreover, he

The Interior of Glasgow Cathedral

became a victim of the Glasgow equivalent of the American Watergate scandal. What happened was that Kirkman Finlay had to secure the favour of those privileged few who were allowed to vote in Glasgow and the burghs of Renfrew, Rutherglen and Dumbarton. Alas, Joe Dixon's father, Provost of Dumbarton, masterminded his son's campaign. And so what did the old Provost do? He took all the voters on a grand tour of Helensburgh, the Gareloch and Loch Lomond, culminating in a wild, boozy party at the top of Ben Lomond. Is it any wonder then that Joe Dixon was returned to parliament.

Kirkman, whose impressive Castle Toward still adds interest to the sail into Rothesay Bay, did much for the city of Glasgow, but just the hint of a dark secret still lingers over his memory. There were those who suggested it was he who planted the moles to spy on members of the reform movement, leading to the hanging of Andrew Hardie, John Baird and James 'Pearlie' Wilson in 1820.

Towards the east end of the crypt, near St Mungo's well, a tomb bears, in beautifully ornate script, the inscription— *'Here Lyis Ane Honorabill Woman'*. [3] Dame **MARGARET COLQUHOUN** of the ancient Luss family, laid to rest here in 1595, would have been aggrieved many a time by the marauding McGregors who raided the Colquhoun lands, stealing their sheep and cattle.

However, she was spared the anguish of the dreadful showdown between the two Clans eight years after her death. For on Monday 7th February, 1603, the Colquhouns and the McGregors met for a peace conference which turned into a bloody battle. The clash happened on the ridge above Glenfruin, west of Loch Lomond. And although only two of the McGregors were killed, *140* Colquhouns met their deaths!

Right against the east gable, in the Chapel of St Peter and St Paul, is the burial place of the [4] **ORRS**, an ancient Scottish family. They owned the estate of Barrowfield. Maybe they could have expected to have a street named after them, which in fact they did, but never in their wildest dreams could they have imagined 'Paradise' coming to the eastern-most boundary of their estate! Well, that's what the football fraternity calls Celtic Park—'Paradise'!

Walk around St Mungo's tomb, looking at the floor. There you will find the nearest burial place to the saint. [5] **RICHARD DENNISTOUN** holds this honour. Dennistoun owned Kelvingrove Estate which, in the middle of the last century, became Glasgow's Kelvingrove Park. This is the park which inspired Thomas Lyle's song, 'Let us haste to Kelvingrove'. It was also the site of three exhibitions, has Glasgow University looking down on it from the north and, on its southern boundary, has Glasgow's Art Gallery and Museum to grace it.

The Art Gallery was built for the 1901 exhibition, by the way. And *no*, it is *not* facing the wrong way round! And Simpson and Allen, the architects, did *not* commit suicide as a result! This particular Glasgow myth keeps growing up again like Kelvingrove weeds ....

Richard Dennistoun's name moved eastward. A huge chunk of Glasgow's East

KELVINGROVE PARK rising up to GLASGOW UNIVERSITY

End became the 'wally-close' district of Dennistoun. Incidentally, would you believe it, Buffalo Bill Cody actually did display his shooting skills here, just off Duke Street, around the turn of the century.

Down towards the east end of the crypt there is a brass tablet to [6] **MOSES McCULLOCH** of Balgray, up Springburn way. Moses died on 31st January 1832, just six weeks before the famous Reform Bill passed through the House of Commons, bringing immense joy to Glasgow. Ironically, Moses would have made a fortune on the night that piece of news reached the city. With people rushing all over Glasgow to celebrate this great occasion with their friends, they would have needed transport. Since Moses operated a kind of taxi service, his staff would have been rushed off their feet, *literally*, for he ran a fleet of sedan chairs!

By the way, it is a Glasgowism that the crypt should be called a crypt, because it is not a crypt. You see, the Lower Church is really *above* ground. 'Crypt' rolls off the tongue more easily.

CATHEDRAL
(*Old Churchyard*)

The Old Churchyard is really much older than the Cathedral, for St Ninian had consecrated a burying place on the green hill above the Molendinar Burn early in the fifth century. It was almost two centuries later before St Mungo arrived to take over this dear green place and build his timber kirk. More than five hundred years passed before the building of a stone structure started.

Interruptions to the centuries-long building operations were caused by design changes, fire, lightning and pre-occupation with wars. A lot of damage came from the vandalism of rebels with causes: but the Cathedral survived the Reformation.

Certainly, by the fifteenth century, Glaswegians of substance were being laid to rest around the High Kirk of St Mungo. But, just to the left of the Cathedral entrance is the classic gravestone of [1] **GEORGE BAILLIE**. Baillie did not regard himself as a Glaswegian of substance: he was, nevertheless, a man of the very best substance.

The great stone is formed like a window—the inscription tells that he was

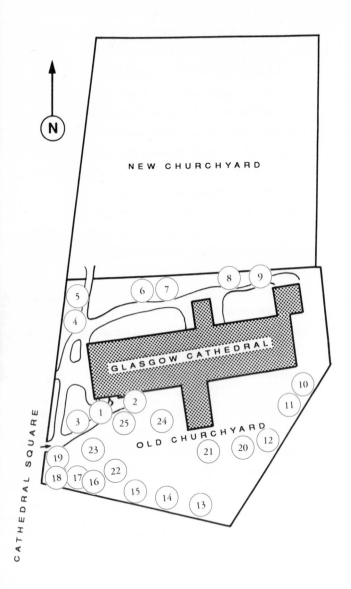

GLASGOW CATHEDRAL (*Old Churchyard*)

a member of the Faculty of Procurators in Glasgow, a sheriff substitute in Perth, and that, in the latter years of his life, he used his entire fortune to set up free public libraries, reading rooms and (would you believe?) unisectarian schools! His stone here tells it all. Imagine this in a multi-sectarian place like Glasgow—and away back in the nineteenth century!

George had said that he was doing these things to 'promote the intellectual culture of the operative classes.' Who knows how many folk read themselves into a richer life because of George Baillie.

A portrait of this remarkable man shows him bearded, dressed in knee-length black coat, tall lum hat and shiny black boots. He looks like the burgo-master in a pantomime. But Baillie was a giant among men and deserves pride of place in this tour through the old churchyard.

On the east side of the Cathedral entrance, another ornate memorial honours the brothers **[2] GEORGE** and **THOMAS HUTCHESON** of Lambhill. They were socially-conscious lawyers in the middle of the seventeenth century who founded Hutcheson's Hospital and School. The hospital stood in Argyle Street until the 1820s and its replacement still enhances Ingram Street.

George Baillie
Glasgow

GEORGE
BAILLIE

It provided food and shelter, indeed a safe haven, for 12 old men and 6 lads who could not fend for themselves.

Life-size statues of the brothers are set into the front wall of the hospital which is a National Trust Office now.

Hutcheson's Grammar School, an institution of renown, has taught many who have gained fame in many diverse careers. John Buchan, who wrote among other books *The Thirty-nine Steps*, and Jimmy Maxton, the MP for Bridgeton, who often upstaged Churchill in Parliament—both were Hutcheson pupils.

Here, just off the south-west corner of the Cathedral, is a flat memorial to the [3] **TENNENT** family, including Hugh of that ilk who was a brewer of distinction.

The family's Wellpark Brewery, the oldest in Glasgow, still brews on. But what would those whose dust lies here, have thought of yon telly ads and lager cans bearing pictures of nubile young ladies? We'll be meeting the Tennents again.

Just past the north-west corner of the Cathedral, a sharply sculpted stone stands over the remains of [4] **COLIN DUNLOP DONALD**. The Coat of Arms on the stone bears a shield, an arm holding a sword, a lion, a crown, a ship and a fish. Colin Dunlop Donald was a descendant of the Donalds who were Tobacco Lords. The offspring of Glasgow's Tobacco Lords were usually given an elegant education and sent round Europe to learn the social graces and gain an understanding of the world. Colin doesn't fit that pattern.

He had a sound old Scottish education, became a lawyer and was Commissary Clerk of Lanarkshire. Yet, despite living through a time when the world seemed to be changing more rapidly than the Creation story, Colin was a stick-in-the-mud. He lit his house only with candles. None of your new-fangled gas lighting for Colin Dunlop Donald. He died in the flickering light of his candles in 1859, having lived for 82 years. The family motto was: *Toujours Pret*. Always ready! Yes, but not for change ….

Just next to Colin is a descendant of another Tobacco-Lording family. The stone for [5] **JAMES McCALL** on the west wall of the churchyard, has a spurred boot carved on it. The inscription reads: 'In Memory of James McCall, Braehead. OB 22nd March 1803 AET 77 years.' The family motto was: *Danger is Sweet*.

What a pity time and tempest have defaced the [6] **BALMANNO** stone by the north wall. All that can be read is: '… Margaret Balmanno spouse to Robert Balmanno.' The family gave their name (with modified spelling) to what was Glasgow's steepest street—Balmano Brae.

Before the street was made, old Mrs Balmanno cherished her physic garden which offered cures for everything from gout to dandruff. Maybe the garden inspired her son to pursue the medical profession. He become a doctor in the early eighteenth century.

The steep Balmano Brae was a challenge, and cyclists used to race up it! But a famous music-hall character called Prince Bendon, at the turn of this century, went *down* the brae, for a wager, on a cycle with no brakes! He survived and won his bet.

Further along the north wall, you are likely to do a double-take when you catch sight of the most grimly realistic skull and cross-bones in the graveyard. They stand out from the stone, carved as if they were real bits of skeleton stuck on.

This marks the burying place of [7] **JOHN TAYLOR** and **JOHN ANDREW**, weavers in Glasgow, with their wives and children. These men were among the last of the cottage weavers and would have left this veil of tears before the Industrial Revolution pulled weaving into the mills. There the weavers, with their fine, individual skills, faded into anonymity. But the Taylors and the Andrews show real togetherness all lying here. They were obviously determined not to be forgotten.

Surely the most mystifying inscription

in this churchyard is seen further along the north wall. Cut into the wall, it reads [8] 'A McKxAB.' Was the carver just a bad speller? Or is the 'x' meant to be a multiplication sign and indicates that A McK and AB did a bit of multiplying? Nobody really knows.

Glasgow has always been noted for its entrepreneurs of the eighteenth century and beyond, but not many of them actually took their enterprise right to the grave. [9] **ALEXANDER SMITH** did. Along near the east end of the north wall, actually fixed to the wall, Alexander's memorial is a sight for sore eyes! He was a slater and tiler, and his wares are here displayed. The memorial is faced with colourful tiles. The sales pitch to end all sales pitches?!

Round now to the south-east wall. There the block of red granite is dedicated to the [10] **MacINTOSH** family of Campsie and Dunchattan. But it must be looked at in conjunction with the huge wall tombstone further to the south. Talk about the writing on the wall—the mon-umental masons must have got writers' cramp cutting the words on this lot! Here lies [11] **CHARLES MacINTOSH** of Campsie and Dunchattan (1766-1843). Charles was a chemist, one of those highly-talented Scots taken for granted by his fellow-Scots, remembered by few and usually remembered for something trivial. Along with Charles Tennant of the famous, or notorious, St Rollox Chemical Works, MacIntosh invented a revolutionary bleaching powder which made them both fortunes. He also devised a way of using carbon gases to convert malleable iron to steel by a short-cut method, and worked out the hot-blast process with James Neilson to produce high quality cast iron. But what do we remember Charles MacIntosh for? Well, he invented waterproof fabrics —the famous rain 'mac'.

Lying here with Charles is his father, George, and his mother, Mary. His grandfather, Provost John Anderson, is also here. Anderson lived from 1635 until 1710 and

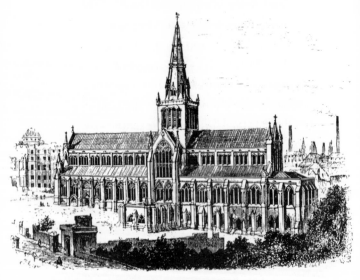

GLASGOW CATHEDRAL FROM THE SOUTH-EAST

the stone reveals that he was one of those 'dedicated to make offer of the Crown of Scotland to their Majesties King William and Queen Mary.' The Provost's father, also John, fills a place here, and he too had a shot at being Provost.

With Ninian Anderson, the great-great-great-grandfather of Charles, and wives, children and other relatives, the family gathering is complete.

Stop further down that south-east wall at probably the saddest gravestone in the churchyard. There you can read about [12] **GEORGE ROGER Jnr**, one of Glasgow's bosses in the troubled 1820s. He died aged only 26. His workers raised this monument to him. To them he was a saintly man.

Now, come along the south wall of the churchyard to the towering twenty-odd feet of monument to the [13] **BELLS** of Cowcaddens. Nine Bells were either provosts or baillies of Glasgow. The stone indicates that the lair is the property of the heirs of Sir James, who was provost of the city. It is dated 1734.

Long before then, in 1640, Patrick Bell was provost and had to go to the parliament in Edinburgh to declare that the baillies and magistrates of Glasgow were fully in support of the Covenanters. This helped to tilt history towards the Second Bishops' War. But in 1679 Provost

Sir John Bell fought on the Royalist's side at the Battle of Bothwell Bridge, and entertained the Duke of York (due to become James II of the United Kingdom) at his house in the Briggait. It seems the Bells were not monolithic. They could certainly ring the changes ....

When the Forth and Clyde Canal was opened in the last decade of the eighteenth century, it was a rare and new-fangled attraction for Glasgow folk in the north of the city. It brought boats sailing past the wee Gairbraid estate to the north-west.

Maybe that's why Robert Craig, a grocer, took a notion to buy part of the estate. He made the purchase of a goodly parcel of land from the owner [14] **Mrs MARY HILL**. Her memorial is on the south wall here, a short distance to the west. It shows that Mrs Mary Hill of Gairbraid and Lambhill has been here since 1809. The contract of the sale of the estate required that Robert Craig should name his newly-acquired land 'Maryhill' to perpetuate the name of the seller. This he did, and Maryhill has grown to become the huge district that we know and love— famous for having nurtured such jewels as Maryhill Barracks and Partick Thistle!

Near to the grave of Mary Hill lie the [15] **MAXWELLS**. The stone on the wall tells you that this is the resting place of

one of those notorious upstart ministers.
The inscription reads: 'Here lyes body of
Ye Revd Mr Robert Maxwell [*now there's a
name to conjure with!*] who served Chryst in
the work of Ye Gospel at Monkton and
Prestwick from 1640 to 1655 when he
was ejected for non conformity, after that
exercised his Ministry partly there, partly
in the city & the country.' Robert Maxwell
got the sack 28 years after the famous
incident in Edinburgh's High Kirk when
cabbage-seller Jenny Geddes allegedly
hurled her stool at the cleric who attempted
to conduct an Anglican service in staunchly
Presbyterian surroundings.

The sharply-cut stone on the wall below
Robert Maxwell's stone marks the burial
place of **PATRICK MAXWELL** and his
wife **BESSY BOYD**. They have been here
since the early seventeenth century.
Patrick and Bessy had a marriage stone
built into the front wall of their house in
High Street. It bore their initials. Well,
marriages were expected to last quite long
back then. The Maxwells had the mansion
of Auldhouse to the south of the city, but
Sir George Maxwell, Patrick's brother,
came into the Pollok estate in 1647.

One hundred years later, Sir John
Maxwell engaged William Adam (father
of the famous Adam brothers) to build
Pollok House. Between 1842 and 1859,

Sir William Stirling Maxwell gathered a magnificent array of art treasures in the house.

Little did he know that, in another 120 years or so, after Glasgow Corporation had acquired Pollok estate, another breathtaking art collection—the Burrell—would be housed just across the park from his.

John Maxwell, another one, was a Glasgow lawyer, but he made his name in 1929 pioneering British talking pictures down at Elstree studios.

{16} **JOHN GEORGE HAMILTON** is buried a few yards closer to the main entrance. His simple stone on the wall reveals his claim to fame: his wife was the daughter of industrialist Henry Monteith. Having Henry Monteith as a father-in-law must have taken some living up to.

Henry Monteith (1765-1848) was the son of a weaver—one of six brothers. By far the most ambitious, Henry ran the family cotton-manufacturing factory in Anderston.

He was also the leader of the group of go-getting young men who smashed the exclusive right of the Tobacco Lords to attend certain assemblies in the city. They threatened to throw him out of the Tontine Coffee Room if he showed his face. He did, but survived to dominate the place.

When William Cobbet, the English

radical, visited Monteith's calico-printing works at Barrowfield, he marvelled at the ultra-modern production line! Henry was away ahead of his time. How on earth did poor John George Hamilton live up to his father-in-law?!

Still nearer to the main entrance, there is the stone of [17] **PETER MURDOCH** on the wall: he is yet another provost of Glasgow. He and his brother, George (who also had a shot at being provost) helped turn Glasgow Green into a sylvan paradise. (If only they could see it now!)

But, Peter Murdoch tried to do much more for Glasgow. Prince Charles Edward Stuart, retreating northward after his Jacobite Rising, ran out of steam and stopped with his army in anti-Jacobite Glasgow. Undeterred the Young Pretender left the city with a load of provisions, boots and clothing for his army. The city had been held to ransom.

After Culloden, Peter lead a delegation to London to seek compensation from the government for the losses caused by the Bonnie Prince's twisting of the civic arm up the civic back. A fat lot of good it did them!

Near the south-west corner of the churchyard stands the elaborate gravestone

PRINCE
CHARLES
EDWARD
STUART

of [18] **Maister PETER LOWE**, surgeon extraordinaire. Lowe certainly gave Glasgow a shake-up. He would surely have laughed at the flattering verse on this stone. He was a merry soul. Errol was his birthplace about 1549. He was a brilliant surgeon and served the King of France before returning to Glasgow. What a shock he got when he saw the state of surgery here!

He decided that barbers should stick to cutting hair and no other parts of the body. His plea to James VI for a Charter to found the Faculty of Chirurgerie was granted. Thus in 1599 his Faculty came into existence to set standards of training and qualifications for surgeons. The Charter was the Magna Carta of Medicine! It's authority brought more benefits— standards for public health and medicines and free service for the poor.

Once Lowe offended the clergy of the Cathedral in some way. It is said he had to stand for a Sunday at a pillar in penance. Lowe burst out laughing during this stint and was made to do it all over again.

The Royal College of Physicians and Surgeons of Glasgow is Peter Lowe's living memorial.

[19] **Mrs HAMILTON** of Aitkenhead lies beneath a giant tombstone of nine pillars and elaborate decoration. Her estate is now the pleasant residential area of

King's Park on the south side of the city.

She was a good housewife. How do I know this? I am told that, but for the ravages of the Glasgow climate over the centuries (she's been here since 1616), we should have been able to read some verse here sculpted in her honour:

Ye gazers on this Trophy of a Tomb,
Send out ane grone for want of her whose life
Once born of Earth and now lyes in earth's womb
Lived long a virgin, then <u>a spotless wife</u>.

Let's move away from the wall now, back eastwards to the low, white tombstone of **[20] Revd JOHN BURNS DD** (1744-1839). He was minister of the Barony Church for 72 years. A stained-glass window in the Sacristy of the Cathedral was dedicated to his memory.

Burns lived in a house just off George Street. His son George was born there. George grew up to own a shipping line, eventually partnering Samuel Cunard sailing ships to the new world.

Incidentally, note how long old John Burns lived. Longevity was a family trait. George's lifespan stretched from 1795-1891.

Grandson John was made 1st Lord Inverclyde of Castle Wemyss in Victoria's Diamond Jubilee year of 1897.

Graham Gilbert, the Glasgow artist,

reckoned the image of the Revd Dr John Burns should be seen by succeeding generations, so his portrait of John hangs in Glasgow University.

Over at the outer wall of the Blacader Aisle, a flat stone covers the grave of {21} **ANDREW MENZIES** of Balornock. He started a world-famous institution in Glasgow—his horse-drawn coaches were the city's first public transport service. He improved on the design of the omnibus which was becoming popular, and invented a foot-braking system which allowed the driver to control his horses with both hands. The vehicles, in Menzies tartan livery, were a familiar sight.

Menzies was the first manager of the Glasgow Tramways and Omnibus Company, a forerunner of the light railway with horse power, which gave way to the electric tram system. This system nurtured a Glasgow stereotype immortalised in music-hall sketch and song—the Glasgow tram conductress—'*Mary McDougal frae Auchenshuggle, the tram con-duc-ter-ess!*'

Move now back westward, but closer again to the south wall and directly opposite the south door of the Cathedral. The large ground-level stone declares itself the burial place of {22} **ALEXANDER COWAN** of Grahamston, Glasgow.

Grahamston was a pleasant country

village where hare and pheasant provided sport. But it changed. Glasgow's first permanent theatre was built there. And the city sprawled out until it disappeared.

That space is now occupied by the Central Station whose bridge over Argyle Street became the 'Hielan'man's Umbrella', the meeting place of exile Gaels. Legend claimed that some of Grahamston still lay below the trains. But, alas, successive searches proved fruitless.

Half-a-dozen Cowans in this grave were doctors. The most famous was Robert, Professor of Medical Jurisprudence in the early nineteenth century. He died aged 49.

Further to the west, near the entrance to the churchyard, is the lair of [23] **JAMES CAMPBELL** of Bedlay and Petershill, under a flat sandstone slab. He was laid here in June 1829, having lived for 89 years. Bedlay Castle was one of his homes.

James Campbell also owned chunks of Glasgow at Springburn and at Dovehill down by the Gallowgate, where East Campbell Street perpetuates his name.

But, out at Bedlay Castle near Chryston, the terrace balustrade is built with stones from that old village of Grahamston where Glasgow's main station now stands. Bedlay is said to be haunted … strange noises have been heard there. No doubt they are made by the ghosts of old actors from that theatre which once stood in Grahamston.

Just out from the west wall of the Blacader Aisle, farmer [24] **WILLIAM BOGLE** was laid to rest in February 1845, aged 84 years. Bogle was a farmer at Papermill Farm, Cathcart. His mark on history was made when he produced a Hiawatha somewhat different from Longfellow's. This Hiawatha was the most magnificent Clydesdale stallion ever to shake a fetlock!

Out in the middle, and a few strides in from the main gate, is the grave of the [25] **BUCHANANS**. Andrew Buchanan (1670-1759) traded in the Caribbean and tobacco colonies of America. He was one of those men who strutted in the Trongate by the statue of King Billy, in red cloaks and powdered wigs. He was provost in 1740-41.

His son George built a grand mansion alongside Shawfield House where Bonnie Prince Charlie stayed while in Glasgow. George called this house Virginia Mansion.

The Buchanans owned estates around Glasgow. Because of their link with the States, two cities in the USA and a suburb of New York share a common name, Mount Vernon, with a district east of Glasgow which was once a Buchanan estate.

Now, let's move to the north of the Cathedral into the *new* burying ground. New? Well, it's only been a graveyard since 1801.

3

CATHEDRAL
(New Churchyard)

Opened in 1801, this graveyard is the
Cathedral's back garden. It's a bit over-
grown, but well worth a visit. Tucked in
behind the Cathedral, it has Glasgow
Royal Infirmary towering above it and is a
car park for the staff of that famous place
of healing.

Three walls, extending north and south,
divide the graveyard into sections. They
help to make it look like a back garden.
By the west boundary wall, a few metres
from the gate, is the grave of [1] **ROBERT
EASTON**, a Glasgow business man, laid
here in the 1820s when the body-snatchers
were doing their worst! Robert's family is
here too. Look at the massive frame of
metal round the Eastons—imagine the
frustration of the Resurrectionists. The
snatchers had no chance! Gabriel's trumpet
couldn't shift this lot!

Half way along the north wall there is
another lot of [2] **MAXWELLS** caged in.
There are even iron bars forming a roof
over them. These are the Maxwells of
Williamwood who intermarried with the
Grahams. One stone shows that a product
of the union was called Maxwell twice!

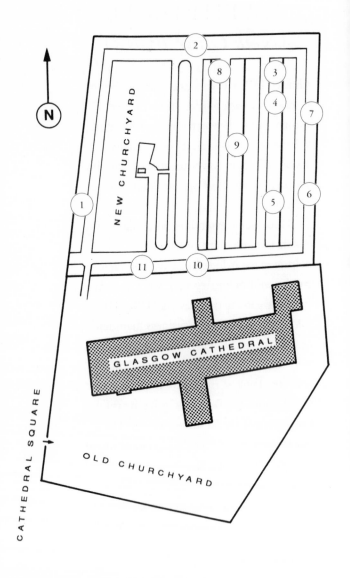

GLASGOW CATHEDRAL (*New Churchyard*)

James *Maxwell* Graham *Maxwell* was interred here in February 1860, at 68 years old. By the way, consider their family motto: *'I Hope For Better Things'*.

There is one rather interesting aside about the Maxwell estate of Williamwood, south of Glasgow—the father of Hollywood film star Stewart Grainger lived here.

Go now to the third partition wall from the entrance. On the west side of it, at the north end, is the grave of [3] **NEIL REID** and his family. The inscription on the wall-mounted stone tells the story of his son, Peter.

Peter was a young bricklayer—just 32. People in Tollcross and Carmyle would see him high in the air in the bright days of June 1818, building a tall chimney-stack at Colin Dunlop's Clyde Iron Works. But, one day, he fell to his death ....

Further south, and on the same side, lies dominie [4] **WILLIAM CHRYSTAL**, born 1776, died 1830. He was Rector of the Grammar School of Glasgow which was then in George Street. In his last years, his old school buildings became part of the famous Andersonian University, and his school moved west to become the High School of Glasgow.

Chrystal had taken over the Grammar School after its teaching standards had been described as shoddy! He transformed it into a lustrous lyceum of learning!

The Andersonian University, of course, vanished to make way for the Glasgow Royal Technical College which, a few decades ago, became the University of Strathclyde.

William Chrystal would surely have been proud to know that his old Grammar School, renamed the High School, would produce two Prime Ministers—the Liberal Henry Campbell-Bannerman and Tory Bonar Law.

To see William Chrystal's memorial stone on the wall, you have to pull back an avalanche of ivy which has covered parts of the wall over the years. And you have to go through the ivy to find the stone of [5] **ANTONIO GALLETTI** just a few steps to the south.

Italians came to this city at the turn of the century and began the glorious mission of energising Glasgow's tastebuds with ice cream and fish suppers. Such superb cuisine remains part of the local staple diet—despite the arrival of newer exotica.

But there were Italians here long before the advent of those bearing chips and pokey-hats. Antonio Galletti arrived here early in the nineteenth century with many more European artists and craftsmen. They were brought by rich Glasgow merchants who wished their mansions to be as braw

as those seen in London, Paris or Rome.
These painters, sculptors, plaster-workers
and wood-carvers were craftsmen of the
finest quality. Their rich decoration may
be seen, for instance, in Lauriston House
in Carlton Place.

Antonio Galletti, carver and gilder,
loved this city so much that he forsook the
warm, Mediterranean breezes for the chill
blasts blowing from Partick to Parkhead.
He stayed on until his death.

[6] DAVID HAMILTON, one of
Glasgow's finest architects, must have
cherished Galletti's skills. Hamilton lived
from 1768 to 1843. Over on the east
boundary wall, towards the south, bold
lettering above his lair declares: *'The
Property of David Hamilton, Architect'*.
Hamilton designed Hutcheson's Hall in
Ingram Street, and re-designed the house
of William Cunninghame, the Tobacco
Lord, to produce the Royal Exchange in
Queen Street. It is now the Stirling Library.
His extensions to Hamilton Palace were
acclaimed, and his plans for the new House
of Commons won an award but were not
the final choice.

David Hamilton seems to have been a
modest man with a happy disposition. He
had a wide circle of friends with whom he
often enjoyed, as Glasgow folk do, a rerr
laugh!

Just a bit further north on this path and by the east boundary wall, a red granite stone keeps the memory of {7} Revd **JOHN ROXBURGH** DD. He was born in 1806 and was one of the stout souls who led their congregations out of the Church of Scotland at the 1843 Disruption. He and his people built their own church—Free St John's—in 1845.

Later they united with Renfield Church in Renfield Street. The church has long since gone, but the name 'St John's' survives. St John's Renfield Church is alive and well and working away out west at Kelvindale.

There's a sad little memorial beside John's. His descendant, Robert Roxburgh, died aged 19. He was a midshipman on HMS Indefatigable. It was sunk at the Battle of Jutland on 31 May 1916.

Now, let's go up to the north end of the middle path.

Many people last century saw things more clearly after they had made the acquaintance of {8} **WILLIAM McKENZIE**. He was 77 years when they laid him beneath this stone on the west side of the centre path, right at the north end. That was in 1868.

McKenzie was the first lecturer in ophthalmology at Glasgow University. He edited the *Glasgow Medical Journal*, undertook extensive research into diseases of the eye, and was a co-founder of the Glasgow Eye Infirmary. His clientele included Queen Victoria.

South from here—about half way down this path and on the east side—you will find a huge granite block at the grave of a man who had a choice of surnames. [9] **JAMES McORAN** or **CAMPBELL** came from near the Lake of Menteith. He died in Glasgow in 1831. A cloud of mystery hangs over that name, 'McOran'. A Campbell forebear of James, back in the seventeenth century, committed some misdemeanour. But instead of obscuring his identity behind a false moustache and glasses, he changed his name from Campbell to McOran.

The Campbells outlived the disgrace and dropped the name, McOran. The names of Sir James Campbell and William Campbell are also here. They were certainly men of substance. Sir James was Lord Provost of the city in the 1840s. He and William were successful drapery business-men. William in particular was a saintly soul who married a lady described as 'the lovely Miss Roxburgh'. Their wedding was a splendid affair of Hollywood proportions, but it is not recorded whether brother James was the groomsman.

Both men had strong social awareness

and did much to relieve the effects of poverty in the city. James had a son called Henry. This lad married the daughter of a rich Manchester wholesaler, included her name in his by deed poll, and thus became Henry Campbell-Bannerman, the first Glasgow man to be Prime Minister.

By the way, remember William McKenzie, the eye doctor? A colleague of his lies down by the south boundary wall. The memorial on it to [10] **Dr HARRY RAINY**, is placed about the middle of the wall. There is plenty of source material taken from the Bible on this stone— three texts in all.

Dr Harry was a surgeon at the Eye Infirmary in Willie McKenzie's time, but, being a really versatile man, he was also Professor of Jurisprudence at the University.

Along, nearer to the graveyard gate, by the south wall, a flat stone covers the grave of [11] **WILLIAM RIDDELL**. He must have been one of the first railway contractors in Scotland. William died at Broomfield in Springburn in 1832, just a year after the opening of Scotland's first railway to carry steam locomotives—the Glasgow and Garnkirk. Could he have guessed that one day Springburn would become locomotive-builder to the world? Maybe not ....

4

NECROPOLIS

Dr John Strang had a dream. The dream was caused by a wide-awake nightmare. In the early 1800s, some five thousand people —mostly Irish and Highland immigrants —died every year in the city from cholera, typhus or other fever epidemics. They were buried in pits behind the old Royal Infirmary and to the north of the Cathedral. The stench must have been appalling.

John Strang was Glasgow's historian through the middle of the nineteenth century and, indeed, City Chamberlain for a while. He considered that Glasgow's 'well-to-do' would wish their last resting place to be in a bright, flowery haven. The Fir Park, the hill across the Molendinar Glen from the Cathedral hill, seemed to John the ideal site.

The firs on that hill had long since gone, but the Merchants of Glasgow had bought it and made it something of a pleasure garden enhanced with elms and willows. This layout helped John's dream come true.

Lord Provost James Ewing, delighted by Dr Strang's proposal, sold it to his merchant colleagues, and the project was

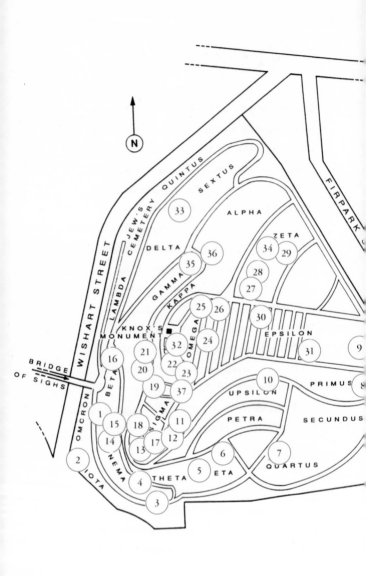

NECROPOLIS

underway. A design competition for the new cemetery brought an eager response from architects.

The winner was John Bryce, who had based his design on the famous Pere Lachaise in Paris. Scotland's first 'hygienic' graveyard was becoming a reality, and was to be special in another way. It would be available to people of all faiths—Catholics, Jews, Protestants ... even those who professed no faith.

The new burying ground, although it was multi-sectarian, acquired a prominent symbol of Glasgow's Presbyterianism. The foundation stone was laid in 1825 for a column which would support the statue of John Knox 225 feet above Clyde-level. Knox stood alone for a year or two, scowling his disapproval at the city's miscreants. He still scowls from the hill-top.

JOHN KNOX

The work was fairly well advanced by September 1832, certainly enough to allow the first interment. This followed an offer from the Chief of the Synagogue to purchase a burial-place. Thus Joseph Levi, former quill merchant in the city, a victim of cholera, was laid to rest that September, the first tenant in the City of the Dead.

The cemetery officially opened the following year. The handsome stone bridge over the Molendinar Glen made an appropriate entrance. The famous burn still flowed through with its solemn gurgle, and Glasgow almost immediately dubbed this entrance the 'Bridge of Sighs'. The Molendinar Burn is now a *culvert* (arched water channel) under Wishart Street which filled the Glen. Glasgow is built on a group of *drumlins* which are mounds with ambitions to become real hills but which never quite made it. The Necropolis is built on a drumlin which makes a neat, square lay-out of paths impossible. The paths twist and criss-cross in rounds and spirals up the mound to reach a more regular pattern on the plateau. Therefore, to indicate the site of a grave is not easy.

However, the planners thoughtfully divided the cemetery into sections and identified each with a letter of the GREEK alphabet or a LATIN numeral. With the ground plan indicating grave numbers and sections, the explorer will, applying some detective work, discover the fascinations of this mountain of memories.

Of course, the view from the north side of the Bridge of Sighs, in Cathedral Square, presents a skyline of rich architecture even before the Necropolis is entered. Some of Glasgow's best architects produced fine memorials here: John Baird, who designed Jamaica Street's Iron Building; 'Greek' Thomson, whose churches still grace the city; Charles Wilson, designer of Park Circus; and J T Rochead, who designed the Wallace Monument on Stirling's Abbey Craig.

Look directly over the bridge to that heavy stone façade set into the hillside. It has a dark central entrance, arched and pillared, with smaller side openings and a thick pillar at each end.

WALLACE MONUMENT, STIRLING

Actually, it only covers a tiny cave where cemetery equipment is kept, but it was built with other purposes in mind. For the merchants of Glasgow intended to drive a series of passages right through the rocky mound to form catacombs for the city's rich dead. This idea died in infancy— the cave is all there is. Nevertheless, the cave was, at one time, used as temporary digs, while the deceased awaited final burial. The Egyptian Vault was used for this purpose too.

Now go over the Bridge of Sighs into the Necropolis, and turn to the right. A short distance along the main pathway, in the MNEMA section, look on the left side to a stone just in front of a wall. Here lies [1] **WILLIAM HARPER MINNOCH**. He lived in fashionable Blythswood Square during the 1850s. His story is not unusual. He fell in love with the girl next door. Their friends and relations were so happy about this romance, but, ah, love was to be blighted. William's girlfriend was arrested and tried for the murder of another lover. But enough of this. The full story will be revealed when we visit another of the city's graveyards. All that need be said for now is that the unfortunate Willie Minnoch has been here since 1883.

Keep going along the main pathway, still with the Bridge of Sighs behind, on into the IOTA section. Look out on the right-hand side. In this graveyard of huge memorials, the stone of {2} **CHARLES WILLIAM FRY** is, by comparison, small.

William Booth, founder of the Salvation Army, declared that the Devil should not have all the best tunes. Charles Fry made sure he did not. He was the Salvation Army's *very first* bandmaster. Fry was just 44 when he died at Polmont in 1882.

Head on round the bend on this path, back into the MNEMA section and look out for the obelisk marking the lair of painter {3} **JAMES MITCHELL**.

What is so remarkable about the resting-place of James and his family is that on this very spot his parents' house stood. Indeed, the Mitchell grandfather resided there before them. For half a century there were Mitchells living here. How apt that James Mitchell lies beneath the place of his childhood, the joys of which are extolled in the verse on the stone.

Make a sharp U turn into the path above where Willie Minnoch lies. A few steps from where the turn is made, and on the left, still in MNEMA, a weather-wabbit stone reminds the world of [4] **ALEXANDER RODGER**—'Sandy' to his pals.

Sandy Rodger was born in Mid Calder in 1784 and came here to stay in 1846. He was in his sixties when he died—not a bad innings for a poet in those days. Sandy was a comic poet, taking particular pleasure out of embarrassing polite society. When George IV visited a tartan-swathed Edinburgh in the 1820s, Sir Walter Scott marked the occasion with his solemn poem 'Carle now the King's come'. Sandy Rodger, on the other hand, marked the occasion with a rather irreverent parody!

Sandy Rodger was a Radical Weaver and suffered for it! Sedition was in the air, and the polis broke into his house and discovered irrefutable evidence of his guilt! The poet's Bible was lying open at 2 Samuel —at the passage which clearly spelled out the duties of kings! So he was slapped in jail, but released *very* quickly—probably because he drove them mad reciting verse!

Sandy's stone says that he was a man

gifted with feeling, humour and fancy.

Turn on your heels now, and walk back round this path into the THETA section. Look out for a Celtic Cross of grey granite in memory of {5} **ALEXANDER McCALL**, Chief Constable of Glasgow for 18 years. He died in 1888, 52 years old. Glasgow opened its grand City Chambers that year. McCall was in charge through some rough times in the city's history.

His profile in bronze adds detail to the cross. Incidentally, there is something very special about this monument—it was designed by well known and very popular architect Charles Rennie Mackintosh.

Move just a bit into the ETA section and look for a small, plain stone marking the grave of {6} **HUGH PERCY FORSTER**, Paymaster of Her Majesty's 63rd Regiment of Foot.

That little stone reveals much of Lieutenant Hugh Forster's family history. He was one of eleven brothers, 'nine of whom devoted their lives and services to their country in the Peninsular War ....'

That war also brought fame to Glasgow man Sir John Moore, who defeated Napoleon's army at Corunna. Sadly he died in the hour of victory.

History might have taken a very different course if Moore and Napoleons' paths had crossed earlier, for Napoleon was in his native Corsica when Pasquale Paoli, the Corsican patriot, round about 1790, threw the French out of his island. British troops backed Paoli up and, as a reward, Britain was allowed to rule Corsica for a while. Napoleon weighed up the situation and, in 1793, decided to join the French. Now, who should arrive on the island just one year later? A British officer called John Moore.

Imagine if Napoleon had stayed in Corsica and had met John Moore. The two great soldiers might have become friends. Moore might have persuaded Napoleon to take a commission in the British Army. There might never have been a Battle of Corunna. And no Forster brothers on the Iberian Peninsula. It's a thought ....

Just here, turn up the path to the right and then left into the QUARTUS section. Look on the right of this path for a bar of music. It can be found on the memorial of [7] **JOHN BELL**. He was born in 1823 and lived only 33 years. The words on the stone are: '*Angels beckon me to the Land o' the Leal*'. Unusual, to say the least.

It is said that, somewhere about here, the nineteenth century victims of virulent fevers were buried in a communal grave.

Keep going along this path, then turn left up into the PRIMUS section. Look for a memorial shaped like a heart. Here lies [8]

GEORGE LENNOX WATSON MINA, a naval architect.

This man seems to have been called to eternity in the middle of a busy life. He designed the royal yacht, Britannia, for Edward VII, after he had produced hundreds of racing yachts for lesser beings. Watson died in November 1904.

Turn left now and go into the EPSILON section to find a great white granite stone, a reminder to the people of Glasgow of a night late in March 1960, when the sky over the city glowed wildly red and orange. Later in the evening, news spread that 19 men of the [9] **GLASGOW FIRE BRIGADE SERVICE** and **SALVAGE CORPS** had died in Cheapside Street, Anderston, when the blazing whisky bond they were hosing, exploded round about them. Here is where they are remembered.

Go back along the path, turn right in the general direction of Wishart Street, and stop just inside the UPSILON section. There is a stone here inscribed to the memory of [10] **JOHN McDONALD**, a Glasgow Post Office letter-carrier, a 'postie'.

John McDonald was 52 when he died in 1882. He was 10 years old when the penny post was introduced. People were, then, still getting used to licking stamps after James Chalmers of Dundee invented the adhesive stamp in 1834.

The old Ladywell Quarry was in this area at one time, and the UPSILON section is laid out along the quarry face. Head along the path with the PETRA section on the left and there, in a crannie of the rock face, in UPSILON, is the monument to more generations of the [11] **TENNENTS**. This family certainly kept close to their place of business—the monument looks down on their Wellpark Brewery. The old family would no doubt be astonished at the state-of-the-art technology which produces the beer and lager these days in a flood well beyond their most fermented dreams.

A little further on, still in UPSILON, is a stone in memory of [12] **FRANCIS FOUCART**, Officer of the Imperial Guard of France, Knight of the Legion of Honour and Professor of Fencing at the Royal Academy of Paris. Born in 1781, he spent 40 years in Glasgow as a fencing teacher. His students raised this memorial to him in 1863. It is worth noting that it was a Dr Foucart of Glasgow who went to the assistance of the Prime Minister, Sir Robert Peel, on a July morning in 1850, when he fell from his horse while riding in London. Peel died from his injuries. No doctor could have saved him.

Follow on right to the end of the UPSILON section and you cannot miss the two-tier mausoleum wherein lies [13]

Major ARCHIBALD DOUGLAS MONTEATH. David Cousin designed this monument in the style of a Knights Templar church. When moonlight glints on it at certain times of the year, it could be mistaken for a flying saucer. It has been here since 1842 and it cost £800 to build.

The Major was an officer of the East India Company, and the thought had crossed more than one Glasgow mind that his wealth seemed excessively out of proportion to that expected of a man of such a profession. But an explanation was forthcoming.

It was said that, during one particular Maharajah's procession in India, an elephant stampeded. The alert and intrepid Major Monteath galloped after it, away into the hinterland. And, you guessed it—he caught the rampaging animal and brought it under control. The elephant's load that day was a casket of precious stones and jewellery, which Archibald took possession of—and kept! He probably thought it was a reasonable fee to charge for his efforts.

Down below Monteath's mausoleum, in the BETA section, are two stones placed side by side. [14] **Colonel PATTISON** was another veteran of the Peninsular War and his battle honours are listed. His likeness on the stone reveals his imposing appearance. He died in 1824 at 39, nine years before the Necropolis was opened.

[15] **GRANVILLE SHARP PATTI-SON** rests nearby. Granville was a notorious body-snatcher! As a teacher in the Medical School of the High Street College in 1813, Granville was just as eager as any other medical man to pursue the current craze for finding out, in a 'hands-on' way, how the different parts of the body all fit together. But in December of that year, he encountered real trouble.

GRANVILLE
SHARP
PATTISON

Mrs McAllaster, wife of a rich Glasgow wool merchant was hardly cold in her grave in the Ramshorn Kirkyard (which we shall later visit), when she was secretly dug up. She was found on the dissecting table at the college. Forensic history was made when for the first time a body was positively identified by teeth impressions.

Granville Sharp Pattison was brought to court, but walked out again a free man when a Not Proven verdict was returned. Two years later, he furthered his career in New York. In that city, one 'G S Pattison ESQU FRCS' was Professor of Anatomy at New York University. He died there in 1851. A year later, his body was brought back across the Atlantic for burial. As far as we know, no one has tried to dig *him* up.

Continue along the BETA section,

passing the Bridge of Sighs on the left, and you will find the stone of Belfast-born {16} **WILLIAM THOMSON**, one of the founders of the science of physics. He added some big words to the English language—'thermodynamics' for instance.

Thomson is much better known as Lord Kelvin. He was barely 11 years old when he became a student at the University of Glasgow, and his great skill in designing scientific instruments was to be the key factor in the successful laying of the first Transatlantic telegraph cable in 1866. He also re-designed the nautical compass and sounding equipment. One old P & O captain called him 'the greatest friend of the sailor who ever lived'. He was 83 when he died in 1907.

Go back up the hill again, in the direction of the Monteath mausoleum, for a look at another monument which is difficult to miss: it is 40 feet high and is said to be built of Irish granite. Standing in the SIGMA section, it covers {17} **WILLIAM DUNN** of Duntocher.

It was said of Willie Dunn that he was so mean that, had he been a ghost, he would not have given you a fright without demanding payment. Born in 1770, he grew up to be a successful industrialist. He had a strange hobby—he took out writs against people, but mostly against his neighbour, Lord Blantyre. The disputes were usually about estate boundaries. In this regard, he was, oddly enough, always most generous to his lawyers whom he kept regularly in business.

On his sick bed, he told a visiting minister that he had overcome his greatest enemy. The minister put up a prayer in thanksgiving, thinking Willie meant that Sin was his greatest enemy. Imagine the good man's shock to learn that Willie had been referring to Lord Blantyre!

Once, when Willie donated only a miserly two guineas to a charity, a friend said to him, 'How mean! You can't take your money to Heaven!' Willie replied, 'I know that perfectly well—it's the only thing I'm vexed aboot!'

Also in the SIGMA section, look out for a small stone which bears the Polish Eagle. Here you will find [18] Lieutenant **JOSEPH GOMOSZYNSKI** of the Polish Army. This exile died in Greenock in October 1845, only 32 years old.

After Napoleon's downfall, the Congress of Vienna in 1815 gave half of Poland (the Poles had been Napoleon's allies) to Russia. The remainder of Poland was to be given self-government. But the Russians denied this to the Poles and so severely oppressed them that in 1830, with a great uprising, the Polish people tried to regain freedom.

The Russians crushed them. Many of Poland's fighting men, like Gomoszynski, fled into exile.

Further into the SIGMA section, in the direction of the Knox monument, you will find the stone to the memory of minister's daughter, [19] **ELIZA JANE AIKMAN**. She was one of those special people who, with their quiet persistence, improve the reputation of the human race.

Eliza founded the Infant Health Visitors Association. Indeed, her work was the basis for subsequent child welfare in the city. Few could have guessed that the quiet lassie sitting on a Sunday in Anderston United Presbyterian Church, would make history. She died aged 77 in 1929.

Just a little nearer to the Knox column, not far from Eliza and in the same section, the [20] **Revd RALPH WARDLAW** has his resting-place.

Ralph Wardlaw was a charismatic personality. His preaching was magnetic. The good, the bad, the ugly, the beautiful, the rich and the powerful flocked to hear his fabulous phrases in his West George Street church. He lived from 1779 to 1823.

A few years after Wardlaw's death, the kirk was sold to the Edinburgh and Glasgow Railway Company and used as offices for Queen Street Station until recently.

Moving over just a little way from the

Wardlaw stone, and as you get closer to being directly under the John Knox column, watch out for the impressive Peterhead granite monument to the memory of [21] **HENRY MONTEITH**. Monteith was that go-getting father-in-law of John George Hamilton whose grave was noted in the old Cathedral church-yard. This entrepreneur owed a huge part of his business success to the genius of a French chemist who left France in 1783.

The chemist came to Glasgow in sole possession of the secret of making and dyeing a Turkey-red onto cotton. He was Peter Papillon.

Peter set up in business, became reasonably wealthy, and Henry Monteith benefited from the Papillon process in the production of his world-famous Glasgow bandanas. These were known locally as 'carters' hankies'. Alas, the Frenchman made the mistake of giving his business over to his sons. The Papillon lads made a hash of their dad's business and the great chemist died in near-poverty in his sixties about 1810. Henry Monteith survived to his 83rd year. He died in 1848.

Come round the path now, not far from Henry Monteith's burial place, and with John Knox high above the left shoulder. On the left side, there is the wonderful theatrical monument to [22] **JOHN**

HENRY ALEXANDER, the most spectacular actor-manager Glasgow has known. The memorial is the stage of a theatre with the final curtain about to fall. Inscribed on the stone are the words: '*All the World's a Stage and all the Men and Women merely Players.*' There is also a verse tribute to 'J.H.' telling that he played many parts, but the finest parts he played were those of husband and father.

Alexander tried to take over the old Caledonian Theatre in Dunlop Street in 1825, but Frank Seymour of the Queen Street Theatre dived in too. J.H. got the basement and Frank got the theatre proper.

While 'MacBeth' was playing in the basement, 'The Battle of the Inch' was thundering in the theatre upstairs. Imagine the clash of noises! Frank's patrons sometimes lifted the floor boards and poured water down on John Henry's customers! Alexander eventually took over the entire theatre and renamed it the Theatre Royal.

But tragedy struck in February 1849 when a false fire alarm caused a panic stampede. Sixty-five people were crushed to death trying to escape. John Henry never really recovered from the shock of that terrible night. He died not long afterwards, a broken man. His legacy was his invention, the Great Gun Trick, brave souls catching bullets in their teeth for amazed audiences around the world.

Close to John Henry's stone, a little further away from the Knox pedestal, there is a fairly big bust of one {23} **DUGALD MOORE**, a Glasgow poet born in Stockwell Street in 1805. He died at 36.

Dugald, as a lad, was indentured to a comb-maker, but his master was almost driven mad because the young fellow was too poor sighted to touch a comb without breaking the teeth! The poor man begged Dugald's mother to take him off to some other occupation in which poor eyes would be less of a problem.

One of Dugald's poems is like a scene from Landseer, the artist who painted 'The Monarch of the Glen'. Here are a few lines of 'To the Vitrified Fort in Glen Nevis':

> *The rising beams of hope may come and gather*
> *O'er other lands—they will not visit us.*
> *The dark stone looking through the silent*
> *heather,*
> *The fort—exclaims, it was not always thus.*

Step now away behind John Knox into the EPSILON section again. John Knox now has his back to the memorial stone to {24} **Sir JAMES LUMSDEN**, Lord Provost of the city in 1866. His dad, also James, was Treasurer of Glasgow Royal Infirmary, and it is said that his expertise at fund-raising was of the most efficient 'getting blood out of a stone' variety.

James Lumsden the elder was Lord Provost in 1843. Earlier, in 1837, he founded the Clydesdale Bank.

Stand looking towards John Knox, then turn right by an angle of 45 degrees. Move straight ahead to the huge statue of **[25] CHARLES TENNANT** of St Rollox —it is just in the OMEGA section. Tennant was 31 in 1799 when he first successfully achieved the manufacture of bleaching powder in his chemical works.

But he was sharply aware of the atmospheric pollution his works were creating and so he ordered the building of the world's highest chimney—450 feet high —in an attempt to lose his fumes into the upper atmosphere. Tennant's Stalk was a Glasgow landmark well into this century.

Over the decades, the St Rollox Works has been one of the city's worst eye-sores, however. Chemical waste was dumped in the Sighthill area causing a deadly spread which local people called the 'Stinking Ocean'. In spite of his chemicals, Charles Tennant was 70 when he died.

This area of the Necropolis is full of industrialists. Further away from Knox, back into EPSILON, don't miss the red granite stone of **[26] ROBERT BAIRD** of Auchmeddon, laid here in 1856.

In the 1830s, the exploration of black-band ironstone in Lanarkshire made that base metal as good as gold. Robert Baird was one of eight brothers brought up on a farm near Airdrie. They had the capital to found the Gartsherrie Ironworks and had become, by mid-century, the largest producers of pig iron in Scotland.

Long after Robert was gone, brother James gave an indication of how rich the Bairds had become. In 1873 he gave half a million pounds to promote the teaching of the Gospel—an astronomical sum!

Over in the ZETA section, there are two memorials facing each other. First of all, look at [27] **WALTER McFARLANE**. His face has been reproduced here. Walter used iron as an art medium.

McFarlane's business began in a small foundry near the Saracen Head Inn along the Gallowgate in 1850, but moved first to Anderston, and then to Possilpark, because of repeated expansion of trade. His beautiful architectural ironwork can be seen all over the world. He produced the frame for Gardner's warehouse, the iron building still seen in Jamaica Street. And his iron lattice designs in the Durbar Hall of the Maharajah of Mysore, are among the finest examples of the art. He used iron as we now use plastic.

Now look at the bust under a canopy

opposite Walter McFarlane's monument. Here [28] **HENRY DUBS** is remembered.

Dubs must be thought about along with [29] **Sir HUGH REID**, who lies further out in the ZETA section. You can reach Reid's grave from Dubs' by turning right on the nearest path, and then left. These two men are famous for encouraging worldwide sales of Glasgow locomotives.

Dubs was a German engineer who founded the Glasgow Steam Locomotive Works in Polmadie in 1863. And in the great Age of the Railway, there were Neilson and Co, Clyde Locomotive Works, Atlas Works and, of course, North British Locomotive Company, first in Hydepark Street, Anderston, and ultimately in Springburn where the Works retained the name, Hydepark. Amalgamations took place until the North British made Springburn the locomotive-building capital of Europe. The skills and experience of Dubs ensured that the Glasgow products were given due recognition as being of the highest quality. He died in 1876.

Sir Hugh Reid was of a later dynasty of locomotive-builders. He was in charge of the Hydepark Works during the heyday of North British Locomotive. Even when he died in 1935, in his 75th year, the works were still sending locos down Springburn Road to the docks. From there, they went off to far away places with exotic names. People lined the streets early on Sunday mornings to wave goodbye to them.

Turn round and go back along this path. Keep straight on into EPSILON once more. There is a stone here over the grave of [30] **JOHN ELDER.** The Elders were a great ship-building family, but son John was of star quality. He was born in 1824, just 13 years after Henry Bell persuaded the Wood brothers to build his Comet. The ship-building skills were in his blood and John grew up to be pioneer ship-builder Robert Napier's right-hand man.

But Elder's greatest talent was his knack of designing marine engines. He designed a combination high-pressure and low-pressure engine which saved 30 to 40 per cent in coal consumption. Ship-owners did not believe him! Only after much coaxing did they buy the engine.

John Elder's name is not only remembered here, but also in the pleasant Elder Park that Govan folk can wander through. A statue of his wife stands there. And there is also the Elder Cottage hospital not far from the Park.

Go further out through EPSILON, close to the boundary with PRIMUS and find a low granite stone with three steps rising on it. Here lie the [31] **PROFESSORS.**

The Dons of Glasgow University and

The 'COLLEGE' RAILWAY STATION

their families, when their time in this vale
of tears was ended, were buried in Blackfriars Churchyard which was close to the
old College in High Street. They were
moved here in 1876 when the graveyard
made way for the College Goods Station.
Railways roared on.

Walk all the way back to the Knox
monument. You will notice, close by it,
the huge granite structure raised to the
memory of [32] **JAMES EWING**, the
same James Ewing who moved the merchants of the city to support the creation
of this Necropolis. James Ewing was twice
Dean of Guild for the city. He was also
Lord Provost, and a Member of Parliament
for Glasgow during 1833-34, after the

passing of the famous Reform Bill.

Writer George Crawford owned a mansion at the head of Queen Street. Ewing bought it from him, with adjacent land, for £5000. A few years later, he sold the lot to the Edinburgh and Glasgow Railway Company at a price of one guinea per square yard. Part of the price was paid in railway shares. A nice little earner!

The house was surrounded by some fine trees and flocks of crows lived in them. They earned for Mr Ewing the nickname of 'Craw Jamie'. Jamie did not hoard his wealth and Glasgow has cause to be for-ever grateful for his generosity.

Follow the path down from John Knox's hill to the main path which runs parallel with Wishart Street. Turn right. Pass the LAMBDA section on the left and you will come to the Jews' Enclosure. That column is a copy of Absalom's Column in King's Dale, Jerusalem. Joe Levi, who was mentioned earlier, was the first arrival here in 1832. By 1857 the Enclosure was closed because there was no more space

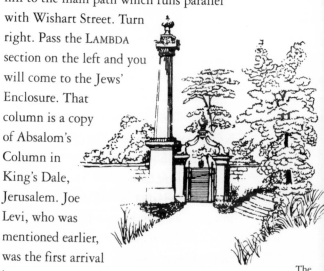

The
Jews'
Enclosure or
Cemetery

available—Jewish people are buried with strictly one body to each grave.

Go back on to the main path and continue past the Jews' cemetery into the SEXTUS section. Move into the terraces, about half-way up the section and you come to the grave of a much loved lady—a Queen in the eyes of many.

Glasgow has always loved fairgrounds (although they were never called that in Glasgow—they were known as 'the shows' or 'carnival'), where the chair-o-planes, the cake-walk and the habby-horses brought thrills and spills into driech city life.

Here, the travelling folk, the gypsies, were always welcome. [33] **CORLINDA LEE** was the Queen of the Gypsies. Her monument once displayed her regal like-ness, but vandalism has struck since she was laid here in 1900.

Swing on up now, through ALPHA, and into the ZETA section again, to find, not far from the monument of locomotive builder Sir Hugh Reid, the grave of the [34] **MATHESONS**. It may be difficult to locate, so look for lair 103. Here lies the **Revd GEORGE MATHESON**, the blind minister who was born in Edinburgh, who ministered in Innellan, and who wrote yon world-famous hymn, 'O Love that wilt not let me go'.

It is said that Matheson wrote the third

line of his verse as, 'I climb the rainbow through the rain'. But the then organist of Glasgow Cathedral, Dr Albert Pearce, who was putting the music to George's words, changed the word 'climb' to 'trace', so that the line and music flowed more smoothly together. It seems that George was not best pleased, but after a while he agreed that the word had to be 'trace'.

Go down into the curving top end of the GAMMA section, and there is the tiny Gothic temple to [35] **WILLIAM MOTHERWELL**, a Glasgow poet, born in the High Street in 1797. Willie Motherwell's poetry often had a Nordic theme, and some of the heroic characters of his verse are carved here.

A fit of apoplexy killed the poet in 1835, thus his transmission to the Necropolis was sudden. For the next 16 years, an old friend came occasionally to pin a snatch of Willie's verse to the grave. This drew attention to the lack of a suitable monument to the poet and eventually public subscription provided the funds for sculptor James Fillans to create this existing monument in 1851.

When Willie's head wasn't up in the clouds above an imaginary Parnassus, he was Sheriff Clerk Depute for Renfrew and the editor of the *Glasgow Courier*.

Hardly more than a glance away from

Willie's Temple is a Greekish-looking obelisk with an urn on top. Here lies [36] **ALEXANDER OGILVIE BEATTIE** DD.

This reverend gentleman was minister of the St Vincent Street United Presbyterian Church (still here) designed by 'Greek' Thomson, therefore it was appropriate that Thomson also designed this obelisk monument to the minister. The stone itself was sculpted by John Mossman, patriarch of the famous Glasgow sculptors who cut most of the stone for the Necropolis.

It would be an outrageous omission if a visit to the Necropolis did not include standing by the grave of [37] **PETER MACKENZIE**. He was the outstanding reforming and investigative journalist in Glasgow during the nineteenth century. He lived from 1799 to 1875.

Mackenzie is in the SIGMA section. (There are so many impressive monuments around this area that you should, in the case of bewilderment and difficulty, look for lair 54.) He organised the soup kitchens in 1847 when starvation and typhus trailed death through the poor areas of the city. And in that ghastly year, he uncovered a vicious meal fraud. A Highland Relief Committee had been formed in the city to dispatch cargoes of meal to help Highland areas suffering famine.

Alexander Bannatyne, grain merchant

of Hope Street, was given an £11,000 contract to provide and deliver the meal. But Mackenzie's friend, Alex Lauder, got wind that Mr Bannatyne was adulterating the meal with 'bran, thirds and sawdust'!

As soon as this news reached him, Peter decided that he and Alex would, that very midnight, slip into the place where Bannatyne's men were bagging the meal for shipment—the basement of the Unitarian Chapel in Union Street. There they took away samples which proved the charge!

Bannatyne was sentenced to four months in jail and fined £400. Then to Mackenzie's dismay, the culprit was released without a fine, and was even paid for the meal! Friends in high places?

As a finale, do look round some of the grander memorials of the Necropolis. For instance, gaze on the largest mausoleum of all. It's in the GAMMA section directly under John Knox, towards Wishart Street, and was built for the **AITKENS** of Dalmoak. It has a domed roof supported on granite columns. James Hamilton designed it in 1875.

The space below is divided into four vault sections for different members of the family. What a sepulchre!

The **DAVIDSONS** of Ruchill have a replica of a Greek Doric Temple on a lower terrace and almost in line with the

Bridge of Sighs. They chose J T Rochead to design it. Rochead's work also includes the building now used by the BBC in Queen Margaret Drive and the Wallace Monument on Abbey Craig, Stirling.

He worked for the Davidsons in 1851, before he went wildly Scottish baronial in style and produced the kind of castle-like buildings which are usually featured in the final scenes of pantomimes.

It is likely that the very first elaborate mausoleum was commissioned by Robert Black in 1837. It was for the interment of his daughter, **CATHERINE BLACK**, who was just 12 years old. It is another Greek Doric temple design close by the William Motherwell monument. The dates inscribed here reveal that five of this unfortunate man's children died before reaching the age of 21.

And what a stark memorial they gave **HUGH COGAN**! Being an elder in the Free Kirk, and founding the first Glasgow Building Society, were among Hugh's life achievements. He was 63 when they laid him here in August 1855.

It is likely that Rochead designed his monument, which stands further round the curve of the path from the Black mausoleum and on the opposite side of Willie Motherwell. Do have a look at it. Its plain, straight lines have a forbidding appearance—four square columns with a top canopy and a heavy base. No fancy urns or faces or convolutions here. Rochead had not yet gone wildly Scottish baronial!

Turn back along this path and go up a flight of steps on the left. Look on the left-hand side, at the edge of ALPHA section.

The mausoleum here resembles a Moorish temple. It would be hard to miss, being domed and octagonal in shape. **Dr RAE WILSON**, a Paisley man, was devastated by the death of his young wife very shortly after they were married. To find some meaning in his life again, he travelled extensively, exploring in particular the Middle East. His book, *Travels in the Holy Land*, tells the story.

Dr Wilson died aged 77 in London and was brought here for burial in 1849. This design by the architect J A Bell would not look out of place in Palestine. No wood, iron or lead was used in its construction.

There are many other fancy façades on venerable vaults in the Necropolis. Maybe the sight of the few mentioned will stimulate the urge to search for more. But, in any case, nobody should bid farewell to this hill of the dead without first returning to the base of the John Knox column.

From this eminence, it is therapeutic to take in the magic views of the big, daft city and its river. And on a clear day, the view may extend to the Cowal Hills ....

On the way down to leave by the Bridge of Sighs, make a short diversion into the LAMBDA section. Just at the corner of the main path with a smaller path is a monument to a man who is not here.

For **WILLIAM MILLER**, former medical student and cabinet-maker, won immortality by writing the Wee Willie Winkie lullaby which has put generations of weans to sleep all over the world. His body lies in a rubble-strewn, unmarked grave in Tollcross Cemetery in the east end of the city. He died in 1872 from a leg ulcer, aged 62.

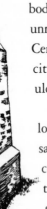

WILLIAM MILLER'S MONUMENT

Some people who have looked on this monument have said that, later, as the lights come on in Cathedral Square, they have looked back into the gloaming settling over the Necropolis and imagined seeing the wispy figure of Miller's Wee Willie Winkie skipping over the Bridge of Sighs.

ST DAVID'S (RAMSHORN) (*Burying Grounds*)

The original Ramshorn Church, built in 1720, was in what was then Canon Street. It had its small graveyard around it, and lairs were sold to defray the cost of building the kirk. The new burying ground to the east and north of the kirk was created by the Town Council in 1780. At that time Canon Street was widened to become Ingram Street, and some lairs were lost at the street frontage of the graveyard.

ST DAVID'S (RAMSHORN) CHURCH (1824)

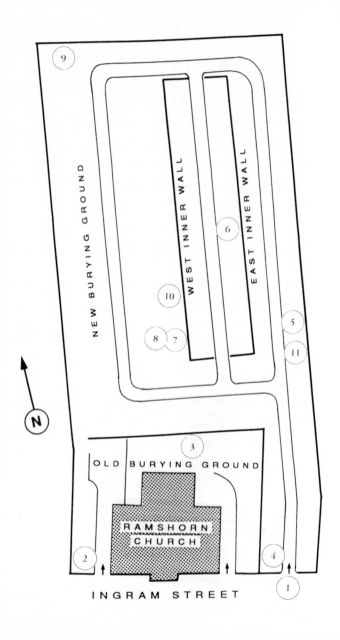

RAMSHORN (*Burying Grounds*)

St David's (Ramshorn) Kirk was the fancy replacement in 1824 for the old, staid place of worship. The architect was Thomas Rickman of Birmingham.

Glasgow then had a Town Superintendent of Public Works, the renowned Dr James Cleland, who decided that he could best do his job by running the city all by himself! Indeed, he took away Rickman's drawings for the new building to a secret retreat—cut himself off from the world for three days—then came back with his modifications. He had added a crypt, and steps to the front door, which folk said threatened life and limb!

That crypt, which became his final resting-place, is still there. And above it, the ornate architecture has a tower which was to provide a 'ring of bells'. Alas, not one tinkle has ever issued from that tower.

Books poured from the pen of Dr Cleland, a prolific writer—books like *The Annals of Glasgow* and *An Historical Account of the Bills of Mortality and the Probability of Human Life in Glasgow and Other Large Towns*. Not particularly bed-time reading!

The first place to be looked at before entering the graveyards is in the street just out from the gate into the New Burying Ground. Grooved into the concrete of the footpath is a narrow cross. Above one side of the crosspiece are the initials 'A.F.'

and on the other side, 'R.F.' The bones of the printers [1] **ROBERT** and **ANDREW FOULIS** were not disturbed when the street was widened. Passers-by have been walking over them for over 200 years.

The Foulis brothers were printers in the eighteenth century who produced work to match the best in Europe. They worked mostly for the University and their volumes in Latin and Greek are superb. Copies are still found throughout the Continent and four are kept in the King's Library of the British Museum. Robert Foulis founded an Academy of Arts in Glasgow, but received little public support. The venture finally drained all of his funds, and after Andrew died in 1775 his remaining assets were sold off in London for a pittance. Robert came home to die in 1776. Andrew was 62 and Robert 69.

Most of the stones in the Old Burying Ground (that is the part immediately around the kirk) have been harshly bruised by time and tempest. But look into the south-west corner at the standing stone of the [2] **GLASSFORDS**. John Glassford of Dougalston (1715-1783) was one of the four young men to whom Provost Andrew Cochrane attributed Glasgow's arrival as a world-famous centre of commerce. The others were Spiers, Cunningham and Ritchie. They were the Tobacco Lords.

John Glassford was a flamboyant, ambitious man who became breathtakingly rich. But while many of his contemporaries lost their fortunes with the onset of the American War of Independence, John did not wait that long to lose his. For he gambled like mad. He would bet on beetles climbing a wall, rarely picking a winning beetle! He even built an outhouse on his estate for his favourite games of chance.

While his colleagues supported Britain in the War of Independence, Glassford supported the American revolutionaries, just to be awkward! He died a ruined and unpopular man.

He owned Shawfield Mansion which sat close to the street named after him—Glassford Street. Bonnie Prince Charlie lodged there in December 1745, during his uneasy visit to the city. There, Charlie met the ill-starred Clementina Walkinshaw, the woman he treated so cruelly—a tale beyond the bounds of our book.

Also in the Old Burying Ground is [3] **ROBERT CARRICK**, a likely son of the manse. Whatever diet he consumed as a minister's son, the part he seems to have shunned was the milk of human kindness. Robin, as he was called, had not one drop of it. He was the meanest man of his time.

Just the manager for the old Ship Bank! He hated passing money out over his counter. His housekeeper and niece, Miss Paisley, was even meaner. She would haggle for an hour with the butcher to get a farthing off the price of beef.

This miserly manager wouldn't even help members of his own family who were in financial distress. One day, however, he got his come-uppance.

Warehouseman John McIlquham, who kept his considerable funds in the Ship Bank, was progressively so disgusted by Robin's niggardly contributions to charity that, one morning, he sent a servant round to the bank with a cheque to withdraw £10,000! Banker Carrick's legs gave way under him! He recovered sufficiently to send the servant back to his master, saying, 'He must be ill! Get a doctor for Mr McIlquham!' The servant took the cheque back and reported Robin's comments.

John McIlquham was livid! He rushed round to the Ship Bank and roared at the Banker that he wanted a £50 donation from Carrick to a well-known local charity *immediately*—or he would draw out *all* his money from the Ship Bank! Carrick made a hasty donation, and, smiling, John McIlquham tore up his £10,000 cheque.

To be fair, while banks were crashing around the city, Robin Carrick made sure that his clients suffered no loss. He was a millionaire when he died in 1821 aged 84.

Now, remember William Minnoch in the Necropolis—the man whose girl-friend was tried for murdering another lover? Well, let's find out more. Just inside the New Burying Ground, on the left, a worn wall-stone marks the {4} **FLEMING** grave. The occupant of this lair, no 5, who has claimed most attention doesn't actually have his name on the stone. He was a clerk from the Channel Islands called **PIERRE EMILE L'ANGELIER**.

Fate nudged Pierre into meeting the daughter of a famous Glasgow architect who lived in Blythswood Square. A fatal attraction flashed between them.

Madeleine, daughter of architect James Smith, began a relationship with Pierre. Her letters to him were passionate and full of promise! But she knew that marriage between a girl of her station and a poor clerk was out of the question. Minnoch, older than her but of good stock, was her official 'intended' and would keep her in the manner to which she was accustomed.

Eventually she tired of Pierre and wanted to end the affair. But he threatened to show her letters to her father and, afraid of the scandal, Madeleine allowed their clandestine meetings to continue, with Pierre slipping into her home without her family knowing.

Madeleine often treated Pierre to a cup

or two of cocoa made with her own fair hands. Simultaneously, Pierre began to suffer spells of groginess. He died in March 1857 with enough arsenic in his body to kill two dozen people.

Now it came to light that Madeleine had been buying arsenic *for her complexion* —or so she said. The obvious suspect, Madeleine was tried for the murder of L'Angelier, but walked from court on a Not Proven verdict. But the scandal was rife. Her father gave up his business and the family fled forever from the city.

William Minnoch jilted Madeleine, and she too left the city for London, where her sparkling personality made her a popular hostess. She claimed that at one of her soirees she served a cup of cocoa to George Bernard Shaw! Later she lived in New York. She died in 1928 in her nineties.

DAVID DALE

Further into the New Burying Ground, half-way along the east outer wall, a wall tablet indicates where {5} **DAVID DALE** lies, a true gentleman whose trade was in cotton.

David Dale was built like a Toby jug. Once, he told a friend, he had slipped on an icy pavement and had fallen all his length. His friend replied, 'Be thankful, sir, you didn't fall all your *breadth*!'

Dale went into the trade of

cotton-spinning and had mills at Blantyre and Lanark. Indeed in 1786 he took Richard Arkwright, the inventor of the water-frame, to see a certain bend in the Clyde near Lanark. This led to the opening of huge spinning mills there.

He was the kindest of employers and the idea of the great social experiment at New Lanark was Dale's, although his son-in-law, Robert Owen, is usually given credit for this attempt at Utopia.

David Dale left the Church of Scotland and formed his own congregation in a church built by his friend, Archie Paterson, a candle-maker. They became the 'Old Scotch Independents'. Dale was their pastor for 37 years. For obvious reasons, that church was known as the 'Caun'le Kirk'.

In spite of being grossly overweight, David Dale, Glasgow's favourite philanthropist, was 66 when he died in 1806.

Move round to the inside face of that east inner partition wall. It forms a kind of closed rectangle with the west inner partition wall. About half-way along the wall, you will find [6] **ALEXANDER GLEN**. There is no particular reason to remember him, but his son, William Glen, has a claim to a morsel of immortality.

Many writers of Glasgow history have assumed that the son lies with the father. He doesn't. Willie Glen was a poet and poor—a hazard of that trade, of course. His heyday was the second decade of the nineteenth century. When Wellington defeated the French at Vitoria, Spain in June 1813, the battle was Willie's great inspiration for the poem, 'The Battle of Vitoria'! Here's a snatch of it:

> *The English Rose was ne'er sae red,*
> *The Shamrock waved where glory led,*
> *And the Scottish Thistle raised its head,*
> *An' smiled upon Vitoria.*
> *Loud was the battle's stormy swell,*
> *Whare thousands fought and mony fell;*
> *But the Glasgow heroes bore the bell*
> *At the battle of Vitoria.*

But probably Glen's most famous effusion was his Jacobite song, 'Wae's me for Prince Cherlie'. Peter Mackenzie, that most daring investigative journalist of the nineteenth century, reveals in his book *Reminiscences* that when Willie Glen died, his rich relatives refused to allow him burial in the family lair in the Ramshorn. Instead he was happed away in an unmarked grave in an odd corner of the Cathedral graveyard.

A stone on the outer face of the west inner partition wall, near the south end, marks where [7] **WILLIAM FRIEND DURANT** was buried.

It is remarkable that two young men who died in tragic circumstances—some 30 years apart—should lie here side by side. Durant, a multi-talented student of Glasgow University, was born in Dorset, and sought higher education in Scotland. A good-hearted lad, he made a host of friends in the city. But illness cut him down at the tender age of 19. Hundreds of fellow students and friends grieved around this grave that day in November 1821.

Just out from William's grave, a flat stone tells the story of equally tragic [8] **DAVID McQUATER**, an apprentice brick-layer who fell from a scaffold in the city in December 1780. He was just 15 years, 3 months old. McQuater's mourners were at pains to record on this stone that David was a promising young man.

Up by the north boundary wall, almost in the north-west corner, you will find the flat stone of the [9] Revd **JAMES FISHER**. He was the first minister of the Associated Congregation of Shuttle Street. They were an intense group and not too happily disposed towards certain Episcopalians who had decided to build themselves a church down by Glasgow Green in 1750.

Andrew Hunter, a master mason who was a member of the Shuttle Street congregation, won the contract to build the 'Piskie' church, but this displeased his fellow members. They knew, of course, that the Devil would be helping to build this church by the Green and told Andrew he must repudiate the contract. He replied with a remark similar to, 'Awa an chase yoursels!'—and was excommunicated!

Indeed, an old woman claimed to have seen the Devil in the 'Piskie' building early one morning—obviously working the nightshift.

The Shuttle Street church has long since vanished, but St Andrew's-by-the-Green still flourishes, not as a church, but as a suite of offices.

Somewhere in an unmarked plot around here, the **Revd JOHN AITKEN** was given burial space. He lodged in the Little Dovehill off Gallowgate in the 1820s. John did not have a church because he did not have a divinity degree, nor had he ever been ordained. His 'cathedral' was the open space of Glasgow Green, where he addressed fairly large gatherings with his thundering eloquence. And what good advice he offered. He would tell his listeners, 'You have three companions you must keep on good terms with: firstly, your stomach, secondly, your wife and thirdly, your conscience.'

He also beseeched them not to be snared by bold John Barleycorn. It was a pity that John himself yielded to tempt-

ation, joining a Glasgow group called the
Cauld Whisky Drinkeronians!? These men all took a solemn
vow never to let *water* pass
their lips. Alas!

JOHN
AITKEN

One last word about
John Aitken. He was often
afflicted by bad toothache
and, especially on cold,
frosty days, he protected
his cheeks, 'chafts' as he
called them, with a piece
of flannel or an old worsted stocking filled
with warm salt.

On the way back out of the New
Burying Ground, glance at a wall tablet
just before passing again the graves of the
two young lads, Durant and McQuater.
Members of another {10} **MONTEITH**
family are interred here. The mother of
this family had 14 children in all. Only
five were alive when she died.

Go along the bottom path and over to
the east boundary wall again. Three lairs
along from David Dale, nearer the gate,
you will find the {11} **PROVAND** family.
Andrew Dryburgh Provand was the last to
be laid here in 1915. He was MP for the
Blackfriars Division of Glasgow.

But, another Provand, George, was a
house-painter in the early 1800s. He
bought the house of the man reputed to

be the richest timber merchant in the city. He was certainly the most ugly. Bob Dreghorn, 'Dragon' as he was called, had a face that turned milk sour! He had the unnerving habit of following young ladies along Argyle Street without actually speaking to them.

BOB
DREGHORN,
or 'DRAGON'

Dreghorn ended up a recluse. His mansion in Clyde Street was close to where the Catholic St Andrew's Cathedral now stands. Dreghorn killed himself in his house—his ghost was said to haunt the place thereafter.

In the 1820s, when the body-snatchers were in full snatch, some daft people looked in at the window of George Provand's paint store, which was just by the house, and saw red splashes on the floor—they thought it was blood! Immediately they decided George was a body-snatcher, although it was not gore on the floor of the store—it was red paint!

They set about wrecking the big house while George ran for his life out the back door. The ringleader Richard Campbell was brought to court and granted the dubious honour of being the last man to be publicly scourged through the city streets! After that, he and three of his cronies were transported abroad for 14 years.

You can leave the New Burying Ground now, to seek the gloom of the Kirk Crypt.

6

St David's (Ramshorn) (*Crypt*)

The Crypt is entered through the offices of Strathclyde Theatre Group. In this dim, dusty chamber, even Dracula wouldn't feel at home. It is partly above ground-level.

In the east wing, indeed, right in the north-east corner of it, a wall tablet does nothing to increase the joy of the visit. It records the spot as the resting-place of {1} **JAMES DARNLEY**, but that is all that can be read of the script. Was it, though, a shiver of black humour which inspired the sculptor to shape this tablet like a coffin?

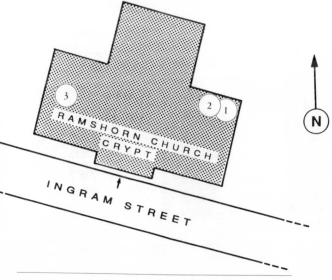

Immediately next to the coffin shape, the sadness of Glasgow man [2] **ALEX BROOM** is held forever in his tablet of stone. Tragedy stalked his family in the autumn of 1827. His daughter, Janet, ten months old, died on the 29th September. And his wife, Mary Rennie, followed Janet to the Crypt five days later. His agony seems frozen into this dismal place.

Over in the centre of the west wing, tribute to [3] **Dr JAMES CLELAND** is made on a large, decorated panel, showing the gratitude of Glasgow Corporation.

Cleland was a builder who helped to surround Glasgow Cross with tenements and shops. But he supervised the building of St George's Church and supplied the design for the new High School of Glasgow without accepting a penny in payment. No wonder the Council appointed him

Some CHARACTERS OF NOTE on GLASGOW STREETS in the LAST CENTURY

Superintendent of Statute Labour—a post
he held for 27 years.

The jobs this man did for the city!
With admirable single-mindedness, he
made improvements on Glasgow Green in
the hard times of 1819-20, providing
work for unemployed weavers; he introduced live cattle-markets to the city, and
he standardised weights and measures used
by city traders.

When he retired in 1834, the city had
a 'whip-round' for him. £4500 was raised.
He kept on writing into his seventieth
year and it was in 1840 that they laid him
to rest in the Crypt he had designed.

But, enough is enough! It's time to get
out of here … lingering too long in this
place could cause frostbite of the soul.

The Ramshorn Church is now a lovely
little theatre.

John Wallace, 'Wee Jamie' Wallace, Captain Paton,
Blind Alick and Lowrie Coulter

7

SIGHTHILL

Like Rome, Glasgow is built on hills. To reach its northern suburb, a long climb is made from the city centre. The journey though, by car or public transport, is only a few minutes in duration. Springburn is certainly high and, within its boundaries, Sighthill Cemetery (1840) is even higher.

The well-groomed entrance on Springburn Road offers a gentle beginning to the uphill walk. What a view rewards the climber who reaches the Sighthill plateau! It is worth a certain amount of huffing and puffing to get there. From this height, the surrounding tower blocks don't seem so towering.

Springburn was the locomotive-building capital of Europe in past days. Now it bears little resemblance to the roaring, clanging place it once was.

The graveyard covers an extensive area, but the burial places suggested for visiting are located on the central hill which is roughly oval in shape. Gravestones here are either obelisks or crosses or great chunks of stone. Only a few evoke the exclamation, 'Oh, look at that!', but the people who lie beneath them are certainly worth looking

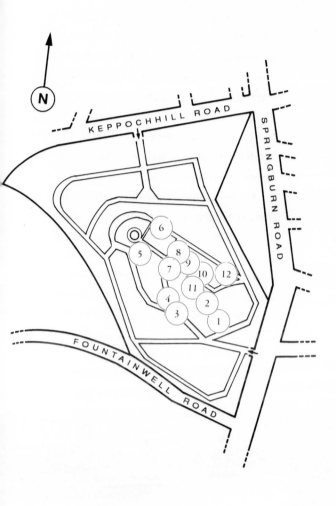

SIGHTHILL CEMETERY

at. They could easily be the players in a pageant of the life and times of a younger, industrial Glasgow.

Just to be contrary, look first at the massive red granite stone of a man who built, not locomotives, but ships. Just a few steps along the main road from the entrance, a path goes off to the right. On the left of this path, a rising grassy area reaches up to the grave of {1} **ROBERT CURLE**. Curle was building ships at Troon when he took the notion to move up river in 1840. Meanwhile a man called Robert Barclay was extending the ship-building business his father, John, had begun in 1818 at the Stobcross Pool near Partick. The two Roberts became partners, and in the following years their names were well known to the Clydesiders.

The Broomielaw, Glasgow in the last century

Their names were a guarantee of the finest ship-building. Their partnership was so bound in friendship that, if you look at the side of this stone, the middle name of Robert Curle's only son is 'Barclay'.

Long after these men were gone, their high standards lived on in the company. In the desperate depression years of the early 1930s, when the Clyde shipyards stood idle and most of their workers were unemployed, a club was formed for the men. Its purpose was to encourage them to take on jobs for friends or local businesses, using their skills to earn a shilling or two. Barclay, Curle & Co allowed the men to use their machine-shops until Clydeside roused itself to the business of building ships again. Robert Curle died in 1879, aged 66.

Climb a few metres up the slope behind the Curle memorial to another great chunk of stone. [2] **JAMES LAURIE**, a Glasgow merchant, lived from 1790-1857. Peter Mackenzie, in his *Reminiscences of Glasgow,* tells great stories about the Lauries.

James Laurie, with his brother, owned a grain store in Union Street. The story goes that once, when the grain was packed into the place up to the roof, water somehow got in and soaked it. It was what you might call a swell affair. The grain expanded to about 50 times its original volume. Then Glasgow enjoyed a unique experience—a slow grain explosion! The store walls and the roof parted from each other in one great belch!

Come back down from that grassy slope to the main road again, and head on with the cemetery entrance at your back. You then come to a fork where you can see the [3] **MARTYRS' MONUMENT**.

From the 1790s, and into the early decades of the eighteenth century, voices were raised across central Scotland claiming that the common people should have a say in the government of our fair land.

By 1820, the voices were getting louder. After a skirmish at Bonnymuir in Stirlingshire, men were arrested and tried for treason. The most celebrated were John Baird and Andrew Hardie. They were executed at Stirling that year.

There is some doubt as to whether their bones lie beneath this well-renovated stone, but it is here that they are regularly remembered. In August of 1820, James 'Pearlie' Wilson, a Strathaven weaver who marched to Cathkin Braes with a ragged group of innocuous 'revolutionaries', was arrested and made an example of. They hanged him in Jail Square, cut off his head and buried his remains in Fir Park near the Cathedral. (The same Fir Park that later became the Necropolis.)

Legend has it that, in the hours of darkness, Wilson's daughter and an aunt dug up the body and wheeled it back to Strathaven in a hand-cart for a decent Christian burial.

Wilson's name was later added to this stone. There is an odd little fact about the Strathaven weaver—he got his nick-name from having invented the 'pearl' stitch in knitting. Interesting.

Go right of the fork at the Martyrs' Monument and look out on the left (five memorials up the slope) for the monument to [4] **JOHN MILNE DONALD**.

Glasgow in the nineteenth century wasn't all crowded tenements and dark, satanic mills. Much has been written about the celebrated Glasgow School of artists in the late decades of the century. But before W Y Macgregor, James Guthrie and George Henry, there had been Sam Bough in the middle of the century. Indeed Sam, who hailed from Carlisle, really took centre stage at that time as Glasgow's landscape artist, and his fame lives on.

John Milne Donald was Bough's contemporary and some of his brilliant landscapes are in store at the People's Palace Museum. He was born in Nairn in 1817 and, as a lad, came to Glasgow to be apprenticed to a house-painter. His boss taught him how to copy pictures and in

no time he was sketching his own inter-
pretations of Scottish vistas.

John Milne Donald spent some time in
London as a picture-restorer, but back in
Glasgow he became a member of the
newly-formed West of Scotland Academy
where his paintings were exhibited. Death
took him at the early age of 49, but his
work became a robust influence on that
later Glasgow School of Landscape Artists.

Interestingly enough, one of Donald's
greatest pictures is not really a landscape
at all. Instead it is of the Town Hospital in
Parliamentary Road.

Continue climbing the hill, around a
couple of curves. You will reach the broad
path of the plateau. It is the long axis of
that oval shape. Turn left and head towards
the circular path at the end. On the left is
a monument which is a sight indeed!

There is no reason why attention should
be drawn to the resting-place of a gentleman called [5] **FORREST** and his wife
MARGARET RISK, except that their
memorial is made of cast-iron in the most
intricate design, and looks like the twin-
towered roof of a church—the rest of the
kirk having sunk out of sight below
ground! Do make a point of seeing it!

Go down the steps on the opposite side
of that circular path from the iron towers.
They are steep—so be careful. At the path

below, turn right and locate on the right the grave of the {6} **MOSSMANS**. The Mossman family have been the foremost sculptors in Glasgow for generation after generation. This John Mossman, who died in 1914, was the son of the firm's founder, John senior.

Few steps can be taken in Glasgow without encountering some Mossman sculpture. For instance, there are the figures of poetry, music and drama on the Citizens' Theatre façade, imposing torsos displayed with a flourish on many commercial buildings, and the impressive likenesses of Sir Robert Peel and Thomas Campbell, Glasgow's most famous poet, in George Square. But isn't it ironic that a family famous for its stony twirls and convolutions, should be remembered here by a simple, unadorned block of granite?

Go back up that flight of stairs to the top path again. The circular path is on the right. Turn left.

Go along to just past another path crossing at right angles. On the left is an ivy-covered obelisk. If the ivy was not obscuring the words, you would be able to see that the stone is dedicated to [7] **JAMES HEDDERICK**. Although sight of his memorial is denied the visitor, stop and think about this man. As owner and editor of the *Glasgow Evening Citizen*, he took note of the comments of a commercial traveller called John Brown. John Brown had written to the paper deploring the fact that, after almost a century after his birth, Glasgow had still not raised a suitable memorial to the famous poet Robert Burns.

Hedderick immediately set up an appeal for funds to do just that. He asked the people of Scotland

ROBERT
BURNS

to subscribe a shilling each. £2000 was gathered after a long campaign and, on 25th January 1877, a statue of Robert Burns was unveiled on the south side of George Square before the high heid yins of the city.

There is an interesting sub-plot in the story. It is said that also present at the unveiling was a man called Archie Campbell, the nephew of Highland Mary Campbell, who was the subject of some of Burns' finest verse. She had died of fever at Greenock in 1789.

Just a little beyond the ivy obelisk, further back from the path, with the circular path receding behind, a true locomotive man is remembered. Superintendent Engineer of the old Caledonian Locomotive Company for decades, [8] **BENJAMIN CONNOR** lived through the heyday of locomotive-building. The Caledonian

Locomotive Company was founded in 1856.

What marked Connor out from other engineers was that he put giant rear wheels on locomotives. They did not turn at such a great speed as the small ones at the front —but they travelled just as fast!

A short distance on from Connor, and nearer the edge of the path, is a reminder of another form of powered transport. The [9] Revd **JAMES AITCHESON JOHNSTON** was minister of Springburn United Presbyterian Church from 1861 until 1895. He died the year after. He was such a friend to his congregation that the church was later named Johnston Memorial.

The manse was Mosesfield house, a fair mansion of a place. From this unexpected location, Scotland joined the motor-car business! For the minister's son, George, was always inventing things, and one of his inventions in 1896 was a dog-cart. But not any old dog-cart—this one was driven by an internal combustion engine!

In partnership with Sir William Arrol, George built the first all-Scottish car. The Arrol-Johnston car looked like a Daimler. After that, there was a rush of entrepreneurs getting in on the act. Our busy roads today testify to this.

It could be said that Sir Harry Lauder was Scotland's first international megastar. He, of course, would have admitted that much of his success was due to the songs other people wrote for him. One of his songwriters was {10} **MACKENZIE MURDOCH**.

Murdoch's cross is found by going nearer to the bend of the path and turning in left over the grass a few paces. Harry Lauder and Mackenzie Murdoch were born in the same year—1870. The former sang and told stories, the latter played the violin and strung words to music.

It sometimes happened that when Harry Lauder was sailing to America to do a show, his ship was delayed by fog or icebergs. Homesick Scots waited in their Broadway theatre, often into the early hours of the morning, until Lauder arrived to perform for them the nostalgic song, 'Hame o' Mine'. It was Murdoch who wrote that famous song and not a dry eye was left in the theatre.

Harry Lauder himself unveiled Murdoch's cross in September 1924. The songwriter had died a year earlier. Those broken fixtures at the base of the cross, by the way, once held a symbolic metal violin. Vandals ripped it off some time ago.

Cross directly over to the opposite side of the path, just about in line with Mackenzie's cross. A heavy block stands above the grave of {11} **JAMES MOIR**. He was a rich city merchant, but his bank account never replaced his heart. Moir was one of the good people concerned for the welfare of his less fortunate fellow-creatures.

He didn't shake the world with discoveries or feats of glory. His public service was as a 'Glesca toon cooncillor'. However, Moir did read avidly and had a magnificent library. And in 1878, just three years before he died aged 74, he gave his entire library to the newly-formed Mitchell Library. He could never have guessed that he was helping to set up the institution which would become, in the twentieth century, one of the finest reference libraries in Europe. A hall in the Mitchell building is called after him. How lucky Glasgow has been to have its James Moirs.

Go back to the long axis path now, and head downhill, round the bend to the bottom of the end slope of the oval hill. [12] **Professor LEIPER** has a squat stone here, right inside the 'V' formed by this path and the one it meets at the bottom. The stone once had a huge angel on top which is probably now on someone's mantlepiece.

The Professor had every right to be proud of his son, William, who also lies here. **WILLIAM LEIPER** (1839-1916) was a successful architect in the city. His fine work can still be seen, like the tall red sandstone building at 153 St Vincent Street, and the Pearson Hall in Yorkhill

Street, used by the Army, which are both interesting examples.

Leiper's career spanned the last decades of the nineteenth century and the early years of the twentieth, but he never really made the 'big time'. He missed his chance. In the early 1880s, Glasgow, recovering from the disastrous crash of the City of Glasgow Bank, wanted to cheer itself up by having a new City Chambers built in George Square. Architects were invited to take part in a design competition. All the greats entered—Burnet, Barry, Washington Browne, Sellars, Young and, of course, William Leiper.

Some jookery-pokery inevitably crept into the proceedings. William Young won, although on sheer technical merit, Browne should have won.

Leiper, however, came in with a very attractive entry. It had a beautiful sixteenth century type façade and could have been a winner. But William had stuck a rather odd, unrelated tower on top. The judges thought it a bit of a joke and dismissed it. William Leiper had missed his big chance.

SOUTHERN NECROPOLIS

Caledonia Road runs off Crown Street in a roughly south-easterly direction and, some distance on, becomes Rutherglen Road. From Glasgow Cross go south along Saltmarket, cross the Clyde, continue on Crown Street and turn left into Caledonia Road. Not very far along, on the right hand side, is the Southern Necropolis.

The graveyard is a huge, flat rectangle divided into three sections. The central section was laid out in 1840, the smaller east section in 1846, and the west section, the largest of the three, dates from 1850.

The heavy stone entrance lodge looks like the gateway of a castle courtyard. It would not look out of place with a drawbridge and portcullis. The central and west sections have paths around their boundaries and centre paths running north/south and east/west. Each has a circular path right in the middle.

The east section also has boundary paths and one path dividing it in two, where it is entered from the central section. Heavy dividing walls separate the three sections. There are no intermediate paths. Visitors to graves in the hinterland,

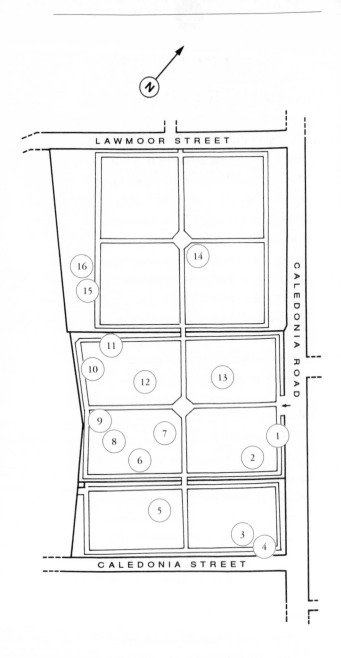

LAWMOOR STREET

CALEDONIA ROAD

CALEDONIA STREET

SOUTHERN NECROPOLIS

are expected to walk on the grass.

Having entered under the arch of the gatehouse, turn immediately left and look for a wall gravestone just a few paces along. The man of substance interred here was [1] **Revd NATHANIEL PATERSON** DD. He died in Helensburgh in 1871. This Kirkcudbright man was 84 years old.

The fact that Nathaniel wrote a book called *The Manse Garden* would hardly be enough to win him immortality. His grandfather, Robert Paterson, however, certainly won immortality because of his nickname—'Old Mortality'.

He was a stone-cutter who wandered around Scotland repairing the graves of the Convenanters. 'Old Mortality' also featured in the first of Sir Walter Scott's *Tales of My Landlord* ('arranged by Jedediah Cleishbotham, schoolmaster and parish-clerk of Gandercleugh'). This was the fourth of the famous Waverley Novels, published in December 1816.

Walk out from Nathaniel Paterson's stone across the square, grassy area for just a few metres, veering towards the path on the left. Look out for a high granite obelisk on a square base. There you will find out about one man who mounted a full scale attack on Scotland's 'curse'.

By the middle of the nineteenth century, this nation's drink problem had already been dubbed 'the curse of Scotland'. Glasgow had certainly made a large liquid contribution towards the problem. But there were some notable exceptions.

[2] **PETER FERGUSON** was missionary to the Gorbals Total Abstinence Society for many years. Those years brought the formation of all kinds of temperance movements. Among them were the Good Templars, the British Women's Temperance Association, the Rechabites, the Sons of Scotland and, the delight of Glasgow weans in the late decades of the nineteenth century, and well into the twentieth century—the Band of Hope!

The Magic Lantern shows of the Band of Hope were indeed magic to the weans who came out of the dark streets into church halls all over the city. A series of slides depicted the plight of some poor family suffering from the endless, heavy drinking of an uncaring father. When he ultimately repented, gave up the demon drink and became a loving husband and dad, the thunderous cheering of the Glasgow children reached a decibel pitch approaching that of a Hampden crowd when Scotland scores the winning goal. Only the penny matinee at the pictures on Saturdays rivalled the popularity of the 'Bandy Hope' with Glasgow's young folk.

The Scottish Band of Hope Union was

founded in 1871 and Peter Ferguson was right in the thick of the activity. He founded Bands of Hope all over Glasgow.

Ferguson died in February 1885, aged 84. He had spent his life in the midst of hope and faith, but probably never guessed that the movement he helped to found would turn out such a success for so long.

But eventually the Band of Hope lost its popularity—like the penny matinee.

Now go through that centre gap in the wall dividing the central and east sections. Cross the central path of the east section to the east boundary wall. Turn left and walk towards the north-east corner. About three-quarters of the way along, move left onto the grass and look for a tall, polished granite stone with a horizontal block of granite in front of it. It is facing west.

The grandest of Glasgow grocers lies here—[3] Sir **THOMAS LIPTON**.

For generations, Glaswegians recovered from, and faced up to, all kinds of crises by making a cup of Lipton's Tea. It made this man a legend. And his Belfast ham was reckoned to be the food of the gods.

His Irish Protestant father opened a grocer's shop in Crown Street in 1849. Thomas was born in the Gorbals in 1850.

After learning the trade from his father, Lipton cut the family ties to open his own provisions shop in Anderston on his 21st birthday. His grocery empire was to become world-famous. Schoolboys would chant:

> *Why does Lipton wear green braces?*
> *Guess! You silly pup!*
> *Oh, Lipton wears green braces for*
> *To keep his trousers up!*
> *That's not why he wears green braces!*
> *No, you stupid clown!*
> *He wears them on his trousers for*
> *To stop them falling down!*

Thomas Lipton's compulsive passion was sailing yachts. He had five of the huge racing type—all called 'Shamrock'—with which he tried repeatedly to win the Americas' Cup from the Americans. He never did, but he had rare fun trying.

Thomas Lipton was 81 when he was laid to rest here in 1931.

In the north-east corner of this east section, a gravestone offers an unusual invitation to read a book. The stone bears the name of [4] Serjeant **JAMES RUSTON**, late of the 94th Regiment. But the real interest surrounds his wife **AGNES HARKNESS**, who also lies here.

On this stone she is called the 'Heroine of Matagorda'. It is suggested by those who have sought to discover the nature of Agnes' heroism, that she was involved in some incident in Mexico. This was probably during the reign of Emperor Augustin de Iturbide, or about that time—probably in the 1820s. Britain would have had troops there to hold the empire-building dreams of the Spanish and French in check. Agnes would have been there with her husband.

The inscription indicates that details of her heroism may be found in a book called *The Eventful Life of a Soldier*. Alas, it seems that no copy of the book can be found, and so just how Agnes became a heroine is still shrouded in mystery ....

James Ruston died in 1834 aged 63, and Agnes was 85 when she passed on in 1856. Will the mystery ever be solved? Perhaps a copy of *The Eventful Life of a Soldier* lies in some attic somewhere, gathering dust.

A modest stone, partially sunk in the ground, can be found by returning along the middle path of the east section towards the central section. A few metres before reaching the opening in the dividing wall, walk a few steps left over the grass. The stone faces south.

[5] **JOHN BEGG**, the son of Isabel Begg, had a famous uncle—Robert Burns. His mother was the youngest sister of the national bard. Isabel was a girl of 11 when she was asked, on her way home from a

sewing class, to stand in as partner to one Matthew Patterson at Tarbolton Dancing School. There she saw Robert Burns dancing with a local farmer's daughter, Ellison Begbie. He was very fond of Ellison but she did not share his feelings. The song he wrote with her in mind does not mention her name, but Isabel Begg told those writing the life of the poet, that one of his finest songs, although called 'Mary Morison', was really about Ellison Begbie.

Isabel told quite a bit of the 'inside' story of the poet. If she had lived in this century, the tabloids would have loved her!

Her son John died in 1867, aged 71. His son Matthew came here in 1897.

Now go through the gap back into the central section, turn left and take a few strides towards the south wall, turn right and walk over the grass a few paces to a solid granite monument facing west. The name of the [6] Revd JAMES SMITH is inscribed here under his father's name. John Smith was a merchant in the city.

James Smith was only 55 when he died in 1857, but he packed a lot of work into his years. He was nicknamed *'Shepherd'* Smith after a journal he edited by that name, and he wrote articles for the weekly *Family Herald*. He also edited another paper for New Lanark's Robert Owen, called *Crisis*.

Some people regarded him as a prophet and were devotees of his volume on *The Divine Drama of History and Civilisation*. He also published his *Family Herald* essays in book form.

By walking from the Revd James Smith's grave, almost in a direct line with the centre circle path of the central section, it is fairly easy to find the stone over the grave of Glasgow policeman, [7] **Police Superintendent JAMES SMART**. He was no softie.

The nineteenth century was barely four years old when James was born. Since he died in 1870, he must have held office through some very turbulent times.

He served at the Gorbals Police Station. Before his arrival there, it was notorious for one particularly ghastly incident in the late 1820s which brought disgrace on an earlier Police Superintendent there. This Master of Police, as the title was then, was one Mr Clark, a cast-iron disciplinarian and Sabbatarian who thought that even to breathe on a Sunday was sinful.

A young Paisley weaver had come to Glasgow for a Saturday night out, got drunk, fought with some ruffians who tried to rob him, and was arrested. While manacled in Gorbals Police Station he fell on an open fire. His screams brought some worthy citizens rushing in to find out what the trouble was. Clark and his surly turn-keys threw them out. Some people went back on Sunday when they heard a man had been burned. Clark locked them up for the night. When they were released the next day, they heard that the young weaver had died. Mr Clark denied all knowledge of the incident.

But the Master of Police got his come-uppance. There was such an outcry that he was kicked out of the job and the local Gorbals magistrates lost their power to Glasgow's Lord Provost and magistrates. The Glasgow Master of Police also took over administration of the law on the south side of the city from that time onwards.

James Smart, however, held the position of Police Superintendent for many

The TRONGATE, GLASGOW, in the NINETEENTH CENTURY

years, and though it is said that he used some old pensioned-off soldiers to fire on the crowds during the bread riots of the 1840s, he otherwise seems to have been firm but fair. He also began a system of inter-communication with other police forces—a sort of embryonic Interpol.

Turn, walk south and look for a small stone shaped like a scroll. It lies a few metres from the south path. **[8] HUGH McDONALD** was the author of the most popular book ever written about the city—*Rambles Around Glasgow.*

In the middle of the nineteenth century, male chauvinist clubs were at the height of fashion. Hugh McDonald belonged to the City Club which met in the Bank Tavern in Trongate. There the

literary giants of Glasgow expounded their theories on saving and improving civilisation.

Hugh was not slovenly about offering advice to young men considering marriage. He advised one young fellow not to bother so much about how a lassie looked, but to scrutinise carefully the kind of washing she hung on her line. A clean, fresh washing was worth getting wed for.

Hugh was buried here in 1860, at the age of 43. His rare blethers ended far too soon—some would say.

Now, here's an interesting connection—it was a chance visit to Helensburgh in 1811 that ensured a place in history for the ship-building brothers, John and Charles Wood of Port Glasgow. On that summer Saturday afternoon in Helensburgh, Henry Bell asked them to build him a steam-ship. It was to be called 'Comet' and would be the first to sail on the Clyde. They decided to take the job and their company went on to steaming success.

The three horse-power engine for the 'Comet' was supplied by [9] **JOHN ROBERTSON** of Glasgow (1782-1868). His grave is down nearer to the south path of the central section, over towards the path running from the main gatehouse entrance to the south boundary wall.

A commemoration plate was fixed to the gravestone in 1912 by the Institute of Engineers and Ship-builders. It records the part Robertson played in producing the 'Comet'. Alas some agency, human or meteorological, has caused the stone to fall on its back. It is hoped that it will be restored to a vertical position again.

Henry Bell, by the way, was not particularly well-off when he ventured on his historic project. Indeed, he never paid the Wood brothers' bill for building his steam-ship—a sum of £100. And he continued to owe £52 to John Robertson as part-payment for the engine. Perhaps these gentlemen did not demand payment because they could feel in their bones that the new era was going to make them 'fairy-tale' rich. Their bones were right.

You now come on to the south path of the central section and walk west, past the centre path, and towards the corner. Look out on the right for a large stone lying on its back. Only the base remains where it was first set.

Members of the [10] **GEDDES** family lie here. The three George Geddeses formed a dynasty.

In 1778, James Coulter, a Glasgow merchant, left £200 to the Royal College of Physicians and Surgeons, the money to be used to set up facilities for the rescue and recovery of drowning persons. Thus, in 1790, the Glasgow Humane Society was founded, and later a house for the Society Officer, and a boathouse, were built by the Clyde in Glasgow Green.

Geordie Geddes became the Society Officer in 1844 and held the post until he died, aged 63, in 1889. His son, also called 'Geordie' by Glaswegians, was Officer from his father's death until 1932.

Drama filled their lives. They were constantly on call to rescue people from the Clyde. Sometimes it was victims of accidents, but more often those who had jumped from a bridge in a bid to commit suicide. The recovery of dead bodies, and sometimes murder weapons, was also part of the Geddes' grim profession.

The third George Geddes, grandson to the original Geordie, joined the rescue business when he gained the Diploma of the Royal Humane Society when he was 17.

On a dreary day in November 1928, young Geordie dived into the Clyde to rescue a man who had jumped from St Andrew's Bridge.

The struggle with the fellow determined to end his own life was desperate. This time young Geordie did not succeed. He drowned in the dark, cold waters of the Clyde.

The whole of Glasgow was plunged

into mourning for that brave young man. He was just 37. The base of the Geddes stone bears the inscription relating to young Geordie's death.

The Geddes family did a job that inevitably made legends of them. It also made a legend of their successor, Ben Parsonage. The Glasgow Humane Society is very special to this city which always raises its bunnet to courage. It is probably the last Society of its kind in the world.

Unless the ivy-clippers have been at work, the likelihood is that the stone marking the resting-place of [11] **ALLAN GLEN** will be obscured. It is west of the Geddes grave and a little north. It is on the wall dividing the central section from the west section.

Glen lived for 78 years until 1850, three years before the opening of the famous school which bears his name, and which was renowned in the following century for its success in science-based subjects.

Allan Glen kept good company—Stephen Mitchell, the tobacco manufacturer who left money to found the Mitchell Library, George Baillie of the famous Baillie Institution, and William Teacher the distiller. Like Glen, they were all members of the Unitarian Church.

The ground for a new Unitarian Church at St Vincent Street and Pitt Street was acquired under the patronage of William Teacher and Thomas Laidlaw, a local customs official. There was a spirited team if ever there was one! The triangular site of the church presented no real problems for architect J T Rochead. His design was in the Greek style. This would have pleased Allan Glen. It being a triangular site, some gesture had to be made to Pythagoras. Allan had been dead for six years when the church opened in April 1856, with no great pomp or ceremony.

For a few decades now, Gorbals children have come into this graveyard hoping to experience the tingling joy of being frightened by the White Lady! Walk diagonally across the grass from Allan Glen's stone, heading again towards that centre circle of the central section, and the White Lady is right there.

[12] **MADALENE SMITH** (not the notorious one) was the wife of John Smith, a carpet manufacturer. She died at the age of 85 alongside her housekeeper, Mary McNaughton, 55. On 29th October 1933, a dark, wet Sunday evening, they were both knocked down by a tramcar on their way home from church.

Mary McNaughton was so much part of the family that mistress and servant were not separated in death. They lie here together, with the White Lady standing by the stone which bears their names.

Children on their way to school on misty mornings can see through the railings of the graveyard when they pass. Perhaps they wonder if yon is a strand of mist floating at the far side ... or the White Lady ... gliding past in the early morning.

North east of the White Lady, about half way between the cross path and the the north boundary wall, you will find {13} **WILLIAM ROBB** who died in 1884, aged 68. There is no special reason that he be remembered, but his gravestone simply has to be seen to be believed.

The base is a dull rectangular block with a semi-circular top to it. Crowning the semi-circle is a huge urn, ridiculously out of proportion with the base. Indeed, if the urn were turned upside-down, it would look a bit like a ballistic missile!

A few of his friends contributed towards the cost of the memorial. Did they mean it as a joke? Perhaps William Robb has already looked down upon the monstrosity and mused, 'My friends ... you must be kidding!' It is surely the ugliest gravestone in Glasgow!

Go through into the west section. It has the same cross path lay-out which the central section has. Walk towards the centre circle and before you reach it, you will notice on the right the gravestone of the Brown family. Two steps further on is the stub of stone which once supported the rest of the memorial to {14} **ALEXANDER 'GREEK' THOMSON**. The top part of the stone has vanished.

Thomson was the seventeenth of 20 children, and became one of the leading Glasgow architects of the nineteenth century. Yet there has always been short measure of praise for his work in the city. Nevertheless, no visitor to Glasgow should leave without looking at his impressive handiwork.

The United Presbyterians engaged 'Greek' Thomson to design their new church to be built on a hilly site in St Vincent Street, and so he created a design which used Egyptian, Greek, Roman and even Indian features. (His nickname—'Greek'—was given to him for obvious reasons.) Experts say that he probably had Solomon's Temple in mind. Crowds thronged into it on the opening day in 1859. The collection taken amounted to a staggering £402.

Also have a look at his Grosvenor Building facing Central Station in Gordon Street; and his masterpiece, the Egyptian Halls building in Union Street which is partly cast-iron. It is a grand amalgam of all his styles.

When he died in 1875, he had packed an unbelievable amount of work into 58 years. The 'Greek' Thomson Society hope to restore his memorial here.

Go on to the centre circle path and walk south to the path which is parallel with the south boundary wall. There are two rows of graves on the edge of the broad grassy margin between the path and the wall. Turn left and look out on the right for a stone with the images of an old-fashioned police helmet, a treble clef and a musical instrument on it.

[15] **CHARLES THOMSON** was a member of the Glasgow Police Silver Band. He must have been looking forward to joining the fanfare as the bandsmen played themselves into the new century, but they had to march into it without him. He died in 1899 at the tender age of 32.

Come back now a few paces to a gap in the double line of graves. Turn onto that broad grassy margin. The back line of gravestones faces south. Move along to a stone almost directly behind the stone of the police musician.

Glasgow in the nineteenth century was not short of 'characters'. They were the street people who scraped a living from performing daft tricks, singing, or making music on all kinds of instruments. [16] **Wee WILLIE WHITE** was one of them.

Willie White was a blind man who played the flute and flageolet around the Glasgow streets in the 1840s and 50s, with a fair degree of skill. He was a squat man, and always seemed to have an expression of quiet thoughtfulness—even when he was playing lively tunes. One admirer said that Willie earned enough to keep himself in 'respectable poverty'.

His Glasgow audiences loved him. They have a habit of taking kindly to underdogs. And so, people were shocked when news spread through the streets that Wee Willie had been taken ill as he tootled one afternoon on Glasgow Green and had died at his Saltmarket lodgings that very evening in September 1858. No one apparently knew what age he was when he died.

Good friends arranged his burial here and had the stone erected. The carving on it is said to represent his favourite musical instrument and the box he carried it in. A fair stretch of the imagination is needed to see it that way. It looks more like a coal-fire, a luxury that Wee Willie White could never have afforded.

WEE
WILLIE
WHITE

WHO'S WHO
IN SELECTED
GLASGOW GRAVEYARDS

CALTON

The name 'Calton' has one pronunciation
in Glasgow and another in Edinburgh.
Edinburghers say '*Caw*lton'—Glaswegians
say '*Cah*lton'. To reach this old graveyard
(1786), travel east from Glasgow Cross
along Gallowgate until the crossing with
Bellgrove Street on the left and Abercromby Street on the right. Turn right
into Abercromby Street and go almost to
the end. The burying ground is on the left.

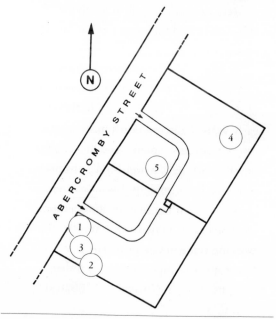

CALTON BURYING GROUND

Weaving was a mainstay of the economy of the village of Calton through the eighteenth century and much of the nineteenth. For a period in the first half of the nineteenth century, the village was actually a Barony or Burgh. Its Coat of Arms displayed three cats with shuttles in their mouths. The shuttle was a weaver's tool.

Manufacturers supplied the raw material which local craftsmen wove at home. Eventually the Weaver Trade Society of Calton was founded, a master weaver's organisation which was really a kind of friendly society.

They bought this area for a burying ground. It opened in May 1787. Another section was added in 1822. Journeymen weavers were not, of course, members of this society, and their families had to buy lairs in the graveyard.

Perusal of the burial records of the Calton Burying Ground reveals something of the state of medical science in those early years. Causes of death make interesting reading—'croup', 'cough', 'cholera', 'fever', 'burning', 'bowel-bind', 'childbed', 'water on brain' and 'decline'.

Just a month or so after the opening of the graveyard, a crisis overtook the weaving trade in Glasgow. The East India Company was importing cheap Indian muslins. This, in November 1786, had caused a price drop in Scottish cloth and a six to seven shilling cut in weavers' wages.

The manufacturers announced that further wage cuts would be made in June 1787. On the last day of that month, thousands of weavers held a meeting on Glasgow Green and resolved not to work for what would be starvation wages.

The strike dragged on for three months. The plight of the weavers' families became more and more desperate. Some broke ranks and took on work at the low rate, and were attacked by the men still holding out.

The Lord Provost of Glasgow and his magistrates received word on the 3rd of September that a crowd was ripping cloth from the looms of the strike-breakers. Down they went to Calton to intervene, only to be pelted with bricks! Up came intimidating reinforcements in the shape of the 39th Regiment of Foot commanded by Lieutenant-Colonel Kellet.

There was a short pitched battle before the soldiers fired into the crowd. Three weavers were shot dead and three were mortally wounded. Others suffered superficial wounds. But the sporadic fighting soon died out and the strike was broken.

Three of the dead weavers [1] **JOHN PAGE, ALEXANDER MILLER** and **JAMES AINSLEY**, were buried here together, just to the south of the entrance to the south section, and by the outer wall. Over 6000 people attended the funeral. The walls had not then been completed around the graveyard, so it was possible for the mass of mourners to spread right round the grave. Two tablets on the wall tell the story of that dreadful day of strife. These are renovated from time to time.

Of the other three weavers, it is said that one was buried in the Ramshorn, one in the Gorbals, and the other in some unknown location.

From the weavers' grave, move over to the south boundary wall and there look for the polished stone of one [2] **JOHN MONTGOMERIE** and his wife, **ELIZA HAMILTON**. It is here, just a few metres along from the corner. These two are not particularly famous, but have a strong claim to be remembered here.

John Montgomerie was an engineer with the Caledonian Railway at Perth. He died, aged 79, in July 1908. Eliza died 7 years before him in March 1901, aged 81. They had been married for 58 years.

The quality of their married life seems to have been unaffected by Eliza being fully nine years older than John. Today, in a society which offers all kinds of publications and agencies for marriage guidance, it might be worth reflecting upon what guided John and Eliza through all the years of their marriage. For it is clearly stated here on the stone—Psalm 23. The Lord was their Shepherd. They did not want. Surely goodness and mercy followed them all the days of their lives.

Just a few steps out from the south wall, and nearer the weavers' grave, an obelisk-type gravestone is a poignant reminder that in Glasgow the graves of young divinity students of the nineteenth century are encountered with sad regularity. [3] **ROBERT MITCHELL** was only 20 years old when he died in October 1846. The 1840s were years ridden with famine and disease. These demons were not selective in choice of victim. Neither saint nor sinner was exempt.

Pass through the opening in the partition wall into the north section and, up near to the north-east corner, look for the modest memorial to another divinity student, [4] **JAMES MUSHET**, who died on Midsummer's Day, June 1819. This was a summer when there were more rumbles of social discontent than thunder clouds.

The inscription on young Mushet's gravestone gives pause for thought: *'That life is long which answers life's great end.'*

Walk back along the diagonal line from the north-east corner of the north section to the south-west corner. Cross the path and look out for another obelisk memorial. It will be of particular interest to Scotland's American cousins when they visit the city.

[5] **Revd JAMES SMITH** DD was born the son of Glasgow couple, Peter and Margaret Smith, on 11th May 1798.

James Smith was one divinity student who survived to undertake a ministry of 40 years abroad in America. He was pastor to President Abraham Lincoln.

He returned to Scotland before the end of the American Civil War, but so high a regard did Lincoln have for him that he appointed James Smith US Consul in Scotland. His office was in Dundee.

You can almost imagine the old minister experiencing such joy when he heard that the Civil War was over; but then grief when he learned how fanatic actor, J W Booth, had fatally wounded President Lincoln with one shot as he sat in a theatre box on the evening of 14th April 1865.

James Smith died in Dundee on 3rd of July 1871. He was brought home to lie here in the Calton Burying Ground.

JOCELYN SQUARE

The visitor looking for Jocelyn Square has to walk down Saltmarket from Glasgow Cross, to the wide space between the Justiciary Courts and the main entrance to Glasgow Green. It is not really a square, but an open area in front of Glasgow's most famous park, with the main road carrying heavy traffic north and south. It is a pleasant place nevertheless, with glorious displays of flowers in spring and summer.

It was once called Jail Square. Now it is called after the old bishop who founded Glasgow Fair. Indeed, this was once the setting of the thrills and spills of the Fair as showmen vied to win customers by offering breathtaking, exotic attractions. The Square also had a more sombre use— public hangings were carried out here.

A stranger would surely never guess that close by this bright, busy place, there is a graveyard. But there is. Some of the people hanged were buried just over there to the north of the court buildings where the City Mortuary now stands.

When the foundations were being dug for the mortuary some years ago, the remains of one of Glasgow's notorious killers were found there. The murderer was an eminent, much-respected doctor with a fashionable practice in Sauchiehall Street. He was known as **Dr EDWARD PRITCHARD**.

Respectable Glaswegians were shocked when the doctor was arrested and tried for poisoning his wife and his mother-in-law. There was also a suspicion that he had disposed of a maid as well.

Pritchard was found guilty and eventually brought out here for what was to be the last public hanging in the city. On that day in 1865, people came from all directions and great distances to be in at the kill. They turned the occasion into a kind of jamboree. Thousands filled the square and the surrounding streets. Traders set up stalls to provide food and drink. People in the tenements around the square let out their windows at three guineas per spectator to enthusiasts who wanted a grandstand view of the final descent.

As Dr Pritchard came out here between two of his jailers and looked around, he expressed his disgust at this outrageous display of bad taste by the Glasgow crowd.

When his bones were brought to light during the excavations, it appeared that he was still wearing his boots. It is rumoured that someone took them as souvenirs!

Be sure that some of Dr Edward Pritchard still lies, with the bones of others, beneath that mortuary ....

GORBALS

Gorbals Cemetery, opened in 1715 and extended in 1807, is quite near the Southern Necropolis. Travel south from Glasgow Cross, down Saltmarket, cross the Albert Bridge over the Clyde, continue on Crown Street and turn left into Ballater Street. A short distance on, turn right into Commercial Road, and the cemetery can be seen straight ahead. The entrance is in Old Rutherglen Road.

The local authority has now tidied up the debris caused by time, weather and vandalism, and the cemetery is now a pleasant little public park.

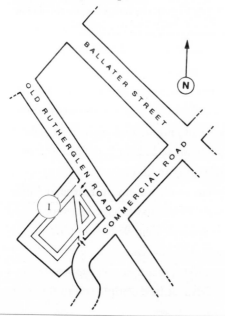

GORBALS CEMETERY

But there are still some gravestones to be seen. Some display the tools of the trades of the artisans who lie here. But, about half way down the path from the entrance, look right and you will see the stone on the west wall which marks the grave of a man who caused Robert Burns much irritation.

[1] **JOHN WILSON** was the parish schoolteacher in Tarbolton in 1785, but the dominie added to his earnings by keeping a small grocery shop. More than that, he sold drugs as well as food, and had a card in his shop window which advertised free 'medical advice'!

Burns spent an evening in the company of the dominie in the spring of that year. John talked on for hours, explaining that he was so skilled in medicine and surgery that even Hippocrates would have been proud of him!

Burns was certainly glad to bid him farewell and get out into the fresh air of the spring night. And as the poet walked back home to Mossgiel, the Muse came whispering in his ear.

The result was his outrageously funny poem, 'Death and Doctor Hornbook', which swept John Wilson into immortality. It tells how Burns, as he strolled in the moonlight, met Death in capricious mood.

Death at first complained to the bard

about Dr Hornbook's (really John Wilson's) magic medicines. The Grim Reaper said ironically that they were so effective, he was being denied his normal harvest of humans! But, after letting out a blood-curdling laugh, Death admitted that Hornbook was in fact killing more patients than he, Death, could handle!

An honest wabster to his trade,
Whase wife's twa nieves were scarce weel-bred,
Gat tippence-worth to mend her head,
When it was sair;
The wife slade cannie to her bed,
But ne'er spak mair.

When the kirk clock chimed an early hour, Burns parted from Death with his mind as sharp and clear as the night air.

John Wilson moved to Glasgow shortly afterwards because of a dispute over his salary in Tarbolton. He continued as a teacher until he took over the position of Session Clerk of the Gorbals parish.

He prospered until his death on 13th January 1839. And he was first to admit that his prosperity was due, in large part, to the interest caused by being the subject of those famous, rather mischievous verses of Robert Burns.

John Wilson's daughter also lies in this grave. She died in 1824, aged 28. Her first name seems to have been 'Campbell'.

Give thought now to **ROBERT HALL**. Liken a Glaswegian to Rab Ha' and you're in trouble. For Rab Ha' was the celebrated 'Glesga Glutton'.

He displayed his addiction to food around the city about the middle of last century. His guzzling was such entertainment that people actually paid for the food he shovelled down his gullet!

He would sometimes leave the city to entertain the populace in the country. There were barns there big enough to house him.

If the *Guinness Book of Records* had been published in Rab's day, he would have earned a place in it for his supreme performance. One day, for a wager, he actually ate a whole calf at one sitting! If Rab didn't feel unwell after that, it is thought that most of his audience did!

Sadly Rab Ha' was found dead one day in 1843 in a hay-loft in Thistle Street, right here in the Gorbals.

Ponder for a while on this extraordinary fellow, and scan slowly around this rectangle of everlasting rest. For somewhere in here lies Rab Ha', his final resting-place unmarked.

WESTERN
NECROPOLIS

Maryhill Road stretches in a northerly
direction from the city towards Bearsden.
At Lochburn Road, a short distance past
the Police Station on the right, turn right.
Beside Maryhill Industrial Estate, turn
left into Cadder Road. It leads into Tresta
Road and to the cemetery entrance.

People come here from all over the
world to stand for a few minutes at the
grave of [1] **Sir WILLIAM SMITH**. A
path from the gate curves round to the
right, behind the crematorium. At that
position, Sir William's lair, K401, is a few
graves in on the left from the path. The
granite stone faces the crematorium. Also
buried here are his father, mother and sister.

William Alexander Smith is well
known as the founder in 1883 of the Boys'
Brigade in Glasgow from the Sunday
School of the North Woodside Mission.
His timing was perfect. The
lads of the city were in need
of something and 28 of them
rushed to join when invited.

So many boys in the
tenement canyons of the city
at that time, had nowhere to
belong to. The 'B.B.' put

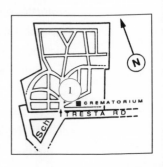

some purpose into their lives. There were games to play, crafts to learn, a uniform to wear, drilling and marching to smarten them up—even wooden rifles to play soldiers with. The rifles were later withdrawn when some folk complained that the organisation seemed a bit too militaristic.

But hundreds and, later, thousands of boys were to have their way of life transformed by joining the Boys' Brigade. They discovered too that they did not meet once a week for fun alone. They would learn that a boy was nearer to becoming a man when he washed some old lady's windows, rather than when he threw stones through them. He would be taught the kind of behaviour that makes Christian principles real.

But William Alexander Smith was not unrealistic. It is said that he believed there was more promise in a Boy daft enough to stick a pin in his pal for a lark, than there was in a Boy piously like an angel! (Interestingly, Captain Smith always spelt the word 'Boy' with a capital 'B'.)

Smith's Boys' Brigade grew to become a successful world-wide organisation to which he dedicated his life. World War I was within a few months of breaking out and he was just short of his 60th birthday, when he took ill suddenly at a meeting in London. He died in St Bartholomew's Hospital on 10th May 1914.

The entire movement was shocked by the news! Four thousand Boys marched into London's St Paul's Cathedral for the memorial service on the following Friday. All the organisations who saluted him as their pioneer sent their leaders—the Church Lads' Brigade, the Catholic Boys' Brigade, the London Diocesan Church Lads' Brigade, the Jewish Boys' Brigade, the Boys' Life Brigade, and the Boy Scouts who came with their leader Sir Robert Baden-Powell.

The night train from London's Euston Station brought the Founder's body home for burial in Glasgow, a city in mourning. Seven thousand Boys lined the route as the cortege came slowly towards the Western Necropolis. Thousands of men, women and children followed. Boys of his 1st Glasgow Company filed past the open grave, each casting a white flower into it.

The B.B. has changed with the times. It is no longer restricted to shrill bugles and skirling pipes. It makes all kind of music now—martial, classical, jazz, rock, folk, you name it.

It is also a far cry from the early summer camps at Kilchattan Bay on Bute, where some Glasgow lads saw the sea for the first time. It is said that one wee lad rushed to tell the Captain the sea had been stolen—it was just that the tide had gone out.

Summer trips nowadays can mean anywhere in the world.

If Sir William is watching his Boys'
Brigade marching smartly towards the
twenty-first century, surely he is smiling.

And now let us move on to the odd
man out—odd man out in this guide
because, although his dust belongs forever
here, he has no grave in the Western Necropolis, nor in any other Glasgow graveyard.
In life as well as death he was considered
odd. **ALBERT ERNEST PICKARD** was
a Yorkshire man who came to Glasgow in
the early 1900s. He bought the derelict
Brittania Music Hall in Argyle Street and
turned it into Glasgow's favourite variety
theatre. Stan Laurel and Jack Buchanan
made their first public performances at
this theatre which Pickard re-named 'The
Panopticon'.

The 'Go-As-You-Please' competitions
—singing, dancing, conjuring, acrobatics
—he ran were glorious fun for those in the
audience and a horrific running of the
gauntlet for the competitors. Not one
aspiring artiste left the stage without
being plastered with rotten fruit! Pickard
also arranged strange exhibitions to
fascinate his customers, sometimes even
displaying shrunken human heads.

He was a rich man and owned a
Kilmarnock Edition of Robert Burns

which cost him £800. He also owned the worlds largest tea-pot, more than 3 feet tall in white porcelain. Later he bought cinemas. His 'White Elephant' in Shaw-lands was considered more posh than the 'Black Cat' in Parkhead which had a legendary resident flea called Rosie.

It is told that one day Pickard went onto the site of a cinema being built for one of his competitors. He asked a crane-driver to lend him a pound. A pound would have been almost a week's wages, so the crane-driver told Pickard, 'By the look of that limousine of yours standing at the gate, it's more likely *you* could lend *me* a pound'. Pickard said, 'Give me a pound and you can have the limousine!'

Those who knew this grand eccentric best, claimed that he would have done such a deal, although the crane-driver was not convinced enough to come up with the pound.

Pickard also stood in a General Election as Independent Millionaire for Maryhill. How bitterly he resented losing his deposit.

He was 90 when he died in a tragic fire at his mansion in Great Western Road on Halloween 1964. He was brought to the crematorium here in the Western Necro-polis and his ashes scattered in the Garden of Remembrance.

ST PETER'S
(DALBETH)

To find St Peter's, head east along Gallowgate from Glasgow Cross for about 120
metres. Turn right into Moir Street and
left into London Road. There is about a
four mile journey along this road (which,
incidentally, ultimately reaches London),
passing the famous Barras Market on the
left, and, further on, passing Celtic Park
at Parkhead, also on the left. About 200
metres beyond Belvidere Hospital, on the
right, turn right into the cemetery.

The cemetery has been here since 1851
and is on the fringe of a place celebrated in
song and story—Auchenshuggle.

Visitors would hardly expect to find a
graveyard in the East End of Glasgow
complete with lines of ornate stone angels,
flowers and trees similar to those seen in
French and Italian cemeteries.

There are no staid overtones of Calvin-
ism here—with one exception. Just inside
the main gate, turn sharply right, and in
the corner by the wall, against a fence, is a
large broad granite stone with, at each side,
a classic fluted column in relief. The Doric
capitals on the columns of this stone have
no French or Italian overtones.

Labour **MP JOHN WHEATLEY** was

buried here in May 1930, aged 61. As Housing Minister in the Labour Government of 1924, his Housing Act provided new municipal houses in clean, bright estates at rents working people could afford. Thousands moved out of the old city tenements to begin a new way of living.

The old method of achieving a full-body wash by crouching in a tin tub in front of the kitchen fire, became a bad memory. The new houses had enamel baths in bathrooms *with toilets*!

Wheatley was an Irish Catholic from County Wexford. His father came to Scotland to work in a pit at Bargeddie and John followed on to become a miner. He was a bright lad—night classes at the Glasgow Atheneum were his escape from the pit.

He worked in a pub, in a grocer shop, he sold advertising for the *Glasgow Observer,* and then went into partnership in a printing firm. But his personality was such that he was destined to become a politician.

Rent increases during World War I led to the famous Glasgow Rent Strike. He was then a Glasgow councillor and joined battle with the authorities to prevent the eviction of Mrs McHugh of Shettleston who couldn't pay her rent. Her soldier husband had been badly wounded in France.

Wheatley won popular support and stopped the eviction. Indeed, his action prompted Lloyd George to introduce his Rent Restriction Bill, and rents were thus pegged for the duration of the War.

However, Wheatley's political activities meant an uneasy relationship for him with the Catholic hierarchy. It sometimes flared into open warfare.

Oddly enough, he was not given a Cabinet position in the Labour Government of 1929. And in the early months of 1930, his health began to deteriorate. Years of stress were taking their toll. He died in Shettleston, his home and parliamentary constituency, late on a May night after travelling from Birmingham.

On the day of his funeral, thousands of local and well-known people alike came together to bid farewell to their champion.

Neville Chamberlain, with whom John had often crossed swords in Parliament, came to pay tribute to a much-respected opponent. Oswald Mosley, later to lead the British Fascist blackshirts, stood by the grave. Beside them was Revd Dr John White, Moderator of the General Assembly of the Church of Scotland, who also came to mark his respect for a fellow Christian.

Continue down the path from the main gate until you reach a flight of stairs on the left. Go up the stairs and along a path fenced with timber. This leads to the 'Good Shepherd' part of the graveyard.

The path bends to the right, but go on ahead, up a narrower path into SECTION 1. Immediately on the left you will find the granite stone above the grave of the footballer **JIMMY McGRORY**. It is the second one along.

McGrory was a Celtic legend in his own time. An old-fashioned centre forward, he looked like a strong man in a circus, with his thick neck and bullet-like head. He represented Scotland in 13 internationals, but it was that head which made him a legend. It could target the ball into the net from two inches or ten feet above the pitch! And from impossible angles! The energy he transmitted to the ball turned it into a missile that even hands like shovels could not deflect!

Celtic fans wrote their own folk songs about him on the terracing … Old men playing dominoes in pubs, still hum those songs, and smile, as they lay down the double-six … They didn't think of him as being 78 years old when they laid him to rest here in 1982 … To them he was still the boy with the rocket header.

Come back along that path with the wooden fences, and down the stair to the main cemetery again. Turn left and walk straight on to the unmade path ahead. It goes through a woodland area.

About 50 metres along, turn right at

an opening in the trees and walk a few steps to a clearing. The line of gravestones opposite are in SECTION 3A.

Look for the large stone at the double-lair of the **GREEN** family. George Green was the foremost pioneer of the cinema in Glasgow. He opened his picture-houses in the early years of the twentieth century when people said the moving picture was but a passing fad.

Green died in 1915 at the age of 54, but sons George and Herbert kept the flicks flickering. They built up their cinema empire which extended from the humble Tollcross Cinema—known locally, and affectionately, as 'The Scum'—to the magnificent Green's Playhouse in Renfield Street, the largest cinema in Europe, with seating for 4400 patrons.

Lads took their girlfriends to the plush red divans in the Playhouse at one shilling and sixpence a ticket—or, if funds allowed, to the golden divans at two bob each! Above the cinema, the ballroom accommodated hundreds of dancers jiving to the dance bands of Joe Loss or Oscar Rabin.

George junior, more often called by his middle name Fred, went to Hollywood on many occasions. He made friends with Charlie Chaplin. He must have had many wonderful memories to enjoy in his latter years. He died in 1965, aged 78.

His mother, Ann, is in this lair, and also his sister, Veronica, the wife of that fabulous footballer whose grave you have just visited—Jimmy McGrory.

In this same line of memorials, just along from the Greens, look for the grave of **Sir PATRICK DOLLAN**.

Paddy Dollan's first claim to fame was staked when he served as an altar-boy at John Wheatley's wedding in Baillieston.

He was a smart lad who educated himself out of the pits. Following a career in politics, he eventually became Lord Provost of Glasgow from 1938 to 1941. He later headed the East Kilbride New Town Development Corporation.

In his early days as political agitator, he once suggested to his fellow-miners that they should demand pit-head baths. They thought Paddy was insulting them! How dare he question their personal hygiene! They chased him for his life!

During the Empire Exhibition at Bellahouston Park in 1938, Sir Patrick had the job, as Lord Provost and first citizen, of accompanying visiting celebrities to the big show.

Unfortunately he was a man with a grave demeanour, and his voice sometimes had a sepulchre-like timbre to it. These characteristics had the crowd in stitches at the Bellahouston bandstand as he gloomily introduced the world-famous Hollywood comedian, Eddie Cantor, to the audience.

The crowd demanded a song from Eddie, who went into a funny routine with his classic *'If you knew Suzie like I know Suzie ... Oh! ... Oh! ... Oh, what a Gal!'* While the comedian danced around Paddy, the Lord Provost remained immobile and dreary of countenance, and the crowds laughed all the harder.

However, in all fairness, Paddy Dollan made good use of his 77 years improving the lot of his fellow man. He was laid to rest here in 1963.

Take the walk back again from the clearing, through the trees, to the main path. Turn right and, in a short distance, you will find, just off the path on the left, a dull, heavy obelisk. There are 61 names inscribed on the faces of this stone. It is in SECTION 9.

On 22nd October 1877, the small town of Blantyre in Lanarkshire was rocked with the shock waves of a mighty explosion. The people of the town knew immediately what had happened. The devastating blast had come from the bowels of the local Blantyre Ferme Pit. Terror swept through the town as families rushed to the pit-head. Before long, the horror they feared was confirmed. Three hundred and ten men had died.

The 61 Catholic miners who perished, are remembered here. The stone displays the names—the youngest, 13 year old **PETER BURNS** … the oldest, 59 year old **NEIL WARD**. This stone tells us about the real price of coal ….

St Peter's is a well-kept cemetery, but away over on the north-east corner of this large graveyard there is a small fenced area known as the 'Bishops' ground'. It is wooded and, over the years, the undergrowth has taken over. The place resembles a jungle. Conditions here make it impossible at present to reach the grave of another East End hero. But a big 'tidy-up' is underway and soon visitors will be able to walk to the grave of **Father PATRICK McLAUGHLIN** with ease. Indeed, his resting-place will actually be signposted.

In 1853 this Irish priest built the first Catholic church in the area at Eastmuir. It was a timber hut. He was popular with the whole community because he offered help to those who needed it without asking which religion they followed. Visiting sick people in the dead of night, wrapped in his shepherd's cloak, local miners along the way—Protestant and Catholic alike—lit his path with their pit-lamps.

Eastmuir was only a small part of Shettleston. Father McLaughlin's parish was spread over a huge area east of the city, extending from the River Clyde to almost the Campsie Hills in the north.

While he was in charge at Shettleston, a thief, with remorse of conscience, came to Father McLaughlin's Confessional and owned up to his crime. He gave the good priest the money he had pinched. Father McLaughlin wrote on an envelope the name and address of the person from whom the money had been taken, and the cash was returned to its rightful owner.

But the police traced the handwriting on the envelope to the parish priest and demanded that he reveal the name of the culprit. Father McLaughlin repeatedly refused, saying that he could never divulge what had been said to him by anyone in the Confessional. He was charged and sentenced to 30 days in Duke Street Jail for obstructing the police. But he served only 14. Bishop Murdoch of Glasgow intervened and leniency was shown. His return to Shettleston was a triumphal procession. An open carriage conveyed him along a route lined with cheering admirers—of all creeds and of none!

He died at 73 after five years of retirement at Rothesay in April 1895. No matter what type of society he had been born into, Patrick McLaughlin would have been that special kind of creature— a good honest man.

CATHCART

From Argyle Street, the route is south,
down Stockwell Street, over the Clyde, into
Gorbals Street and on to Cathcart Road.
After about two miles, turn left into
Holmlea Road which eventually becomes
Clarkston Road. Turn left into Brenfield
Road and look out for the graveyard on
the right. Through the main gate, a wide
forecourt stretches in front of a lodge
house which has seen better days. Take the
road to the left and continue round a long
sweeping curve which rises as it goes.

Where it begins to level off, the small
M SECTION of the graveyard is on the left.

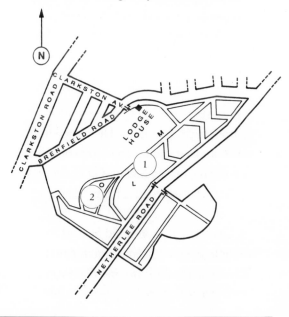

CATHCART CEMETERY

At the end of the section, an area is used for refuse collection. Look out now on the left side of the road to the first line of gravestones in from the road edge. You face the gravestone of the [1] **MACKIE** family. This is L SECTION and the Mackie stone is marked L204. The unmarked grave to the left of it is lair L203.

In this grave lies a lady professional singer called **MADGE METCALFE**. She was buried here in December 1908, aged 50, still in her prime. The records state that she died of 'debility'.

Madge Metcalfe's married name was 'Jefferson'. Her husband Arthur, a native of Ulverston in Cumberland, brought his family to Glasgow after a stay in Bishop Auckland. A man of the theatre, he became manager of the Scotia Music Hall in Stockwell Street, later known as the 'Metrople'.

The Jefferson son, Stanley, couldn't wait to slap on the greasepaint and get out in front of the footlights. He fancied himself as a singer, dancer and light comedian. But no amount of pleading would persuade Arthur Jefferson to give his son a spot in the show.

Undeterred, 16 year old Stanley went along to the rival Panopticon in Argyle Street and asked its owner—A E Pickard, whom we have already met—for a job.

Pickard said yes and young Stanley had his first ever professional performance. He was a smash hit! And there was to be no looking back. And thus the show-biz career of one Stan Laurel, complete with new stage name, took off. This was many years, of course, before the immortal pairing of Stan Laurel with Oliver Hardy.

Questions still linger over the grave of Stan Laurel's mother. Why was no stone ever set here to mark her final resting-place? Did the great Hollywood star ever get a chance to stand for a quiet moment or two at her graveside during his fleeting visit to Glasgow mobbed by cheering fans. Why, as it seems, was she forgotten?

Move on along this road to a point where it divides into three narrower roads. Go up the middle one up to the top of the hill. On the right is the O SECTION.

Walk down a grassy path, on the right, to the fourth line of gravestones on the left. There you will find a large wide granite stone facing the path. Here rest the [2] McCOLLS. The most famous was **ROBERT S McCOLL** who died in 1958, aged 82. He played amateur football with Queens Park, but he was so good that Newcastle United snapped him up and made him a professional. But he was still with Queens Park when he earned his first international cap in March, 1896 against

Wales, aged 20. He won 13 full caps in all.

After Newcastle he joined Rangers, earning the title of 'King of all centre-forwards'. However, in the 1906-7 season he astonished the football world by returning to the amateur ranks with his old club, Queens Park.

Football was not Bob McColl's only claim to fame. He and his brother, Thomas, who also lies here, must have sensed that there was profit to be made exploiting Glasgow's notorious sweet tooth. So they opened a 'sweetie' factory.

In Glasgow, confections are never called just 'sweets' or 'candy'—sweets in this city are given exotic names, from 'conversation lozenges' to 'chocolate drops' to 'hazelnut whirls'. The McColls opened shops to retail their luscious joys. In the days when cinema-going was a main Glasgow pastime, few patrons would think about going into the box-office without first dropping in at R S McColl's for a poke of sweeties. Even the addict would keep some back for the 'big' picture.

Perhaps Glasgow dentists ought to get together sometime to arrange a pilgrim-age to the McColl grave, by way of giving thanks for the business the sweetie-sooking McColl customers must have put their way.

St Kentigern's

From George Square, you go up North Hanover Street until the Buchanan Street Bus Station appears on the left. Turn left into Cowcaddens Road. The bus station is still on the left and the Glasgow College is on the right. Further on, Cowcaddens becomes Garscube Road. At a set of traffic lights, fork right into Possil Road and go on to turn left into Saracen Street. Stay on it—it is a long, straight thoroughfare, but, with a couple of curves at its far end, it becomes Balmore Road.

Balmore Road takes a fairly lengthy trip through Lambhill, which is just another thickly-populated suburb of the city—on its north-western edge. Suddenly it stops being thickly-populated and the traveller is out there, moving across wide, open country.

Not far from the end of the built-up part of Lambhill, turn left in through the cemetery entrance. Row upon row of gravestones go on as far as the eye can see. They support a huge host of white angels and saints which give the place a touch of Italian or French—a bit like St Peter's cemetery in the south east, but more open.

Walk up the main road from the entrance and turn left into the third path along. Continue up the rise almost to the next cross path. Look a few degrees to the right and you will find a dark stone carrying an inscription in gilt lettering.

Here, in SECTION 15, is the grave of yet another Glasgow legend. Many sit in pubs and clubs still claiming even the most tenuous link with boxer **BENNY LYNCH**. Even having a granny whose milkman once met the wee champ is a valid enough boast.

The Lynch family came from Ireland in the late nineteenth century, at a time when the poverty endured over there made the notion of moving to Glasgow seem like a trip to the Promised Land.

They settled in the Gorbals where Benny Lynch was born in 1913. Life was a struggle for most people in the Gorbals back then, but Benny had something to offer. He showed the local boxing fraternity that he could fight for his living in the ring—better than most of the lads in the game.

Around the booths and boxing arenas, his reputation grew, and, by the mid-thirties he had taken the flyweight crown from Jackie Brown in Manchester. The Americans, however, did not recognise him as undisputed world flyweight champion until he beat their lad, Small Montana, in London.

Glasgow went quite hysterical over its new world champion—the first that Scotland had ever had. Citizens claimed that his fists travelled faster than the speed of light! He was never allowed to escape from the glaring spotlight of publicity or entertainment.

But alas, in a year or so, the demon drink began to take the fine, sharp edge off the champ. His training was not going well and fat was growing around his muscles.

In June 1938, he was due to defend his title against the American, Jackie Jurich, at Shawfield Park. Now it happened that, at this time, the bridge which carried trains from the Central Station across the Clyde had a huge advertisement plastered across it. The ad was for a well-known cheap wine and it claimed that there were 'six-and-a-half pounds of grapes in every bottle'.

At the weigh-in before the big fight, the unfortunate Benny Lynch was found to be exactly *six-and-a-half pounds overweight.*

Naturally the cynics made a lot of the coincidence. The weight gain had cost Lynch his title. The fight went on at catch-weights with no title at stake. Ironically Lynch won easily, but from then on his journey was downhill. The drink was beating him.

Sir Harry Lauder, a keen supporter of boxing, tried to talk Benny into giving up drink. But the wee fellow told him, 'I was born in the gutter and I'll die in the gutter'.

One July evening in 1946, at a particularly dull boxing gala in Hampden Park, the fans were booing and on the point of leaving when Benny Lynch shuffled down to a ring-side seat someone had bought for him. When he was spotted, thunderous cheering swept round the arena in a warm tribute to him. It was his last ovation. He died days later on the 6th of August.

This stone, erected by his fans, looks over to the Campsie hills where Benny jogged, training for his fights. The stone bears an etched likeness of him in boxing gear and calls him the 'Undefeated World Flyweight Champion'.

This is not strictly true perhaps. He was defeated—by the broken parts of his personality, by the relentless adoration, by life itself. But in the folk memory of this city, Benny Lynch will always be undefeated.

Epilogue

They wove all kinds of colours
Through this city,
In their years:
The righteous, the ridiculous, the giants
    and the just.
They scared it out its senses,
Made it giggle,
Dried its tears,
Until, into its quiet places, Glasgow
    wove their dust.

BIBLIOGRAPHY

Barr, William W, *Glaswegiana*, Glasgow: Vista, 1972.

Cowan, James, *From Glasgow's Treasure Chest*, Glasgow: Craig Wilson, 1951.

Glasgow's Glasgow, People within a City, Glasgow: The Words and the Stones, 1990.

Mackenzie, Peter, *Old Reminiscences and Remarkable Characters of Glasgow*, Glasgow: James P Forrester 1875.

Simpson, William, *Glasgow in the 'Forties,* Glasgow: Morison Bros, 1899.

Stuart, Andy, Old Springburn, Glasgow: Richard Stenlake, 1982.

Waugh, Thomas M, *Shettleston from Old and New Photographs*, Sandyhill East Community Council, 1986.

Willing, June A and J Scott Fairie, *Burial Grounds of Glasgow*, Glasgow and West of Scotland Family History Society, 1986.